THE FLOWING TIDE
More Irish Set Dancing

Pat Murphy

MERCIER PRESS

Published in 2000 by
Mercier Press
5 French Church Street Cork
Tel: (021) 275040; Fax (021) 274969
E-mail: books@mercier.ie
16 Hume Street Dublin 2
Tel: (01) 661 5299; Fax: (01) 661 8583
E-mail: books@marino.ie

Trade enquiries to CMD Distribution 55A Spruce Avenue Stillorgan Industrial Park Blackrock
County Dublin
Tel: (01) 294 2556; Fax: (01) 294 2564
E-mail: cmd@columba.ie

© Pat Murphy

ISBN 1 85635 308 7

10 9 8 7 6 5 4 3 2 1

A CIP record for this title is available from the British Library
Cover design by Penhouse Design Group
Typeset by Deirdre's Desktop
Printed in Ireland by Cox & Wyman Reading Berks

*This book is dedicated to the memory of set dancing master
Connie Ryan.*

CONTENTS

ACKNOWLEDGEMENTS

Once again I wish to thank the many friends whose help and encouragement made this second book of set dances possible. When *Toss the Feathers* was published almost five years ago, it was a dream come true. At that time, it did not occur to me that I would ever have enough other sets to make a second book possible. The dancing revival has continued, however, and I feel privileged to have had the opportunity of learning so many more dances and putting this new collection together.

As before, so many people contributed in different ways to the making of the book that I worry about leaving somebody out. It is sad to think that some of those special people who helped me have now passed away. My thanks to all of the following, who shared their knowledge and dances with me: Connie Ryan, Jer MacAuliffe, Frank Roddy, Geoff Holland, Eileen O'Doherty, Betty McCoy, Elizabeth MacDonald, Mickey Kelly, Olive Lynch, Jean Ver Hoeven, Ciarán Condron, Seamus Ó Méalóid, Timmy MacCarthy, Josie O'Rourke, Jack Grogan, Nora Carroll, Aidan Vaughan, Micheál Ó hAlmhaín, Marie Philbin, Anna Pegley, Mary Whyte, Miley Costelloe, Brenda O'Callaghan, Mick Mulkerrin, Eamon Gannon, Maureen Culleton, Matt Cunningham, Bridget May, Martin Bolger, Martin Murray, Mick and Mary Corcoran, Aleta Hancock, Brendan and Eileen Reilly, Carmel O'Callaghan, Mary Walshe, John O'Connor, Paddy Hanafin, Brigid Collins, Tommy Gannon, Gerry O'Sullivan, Angela Bernard, Mary Gohery, Anne O'Donnell and Carmel Kearns.

Special thanks to Elizabeth MacDonald, Bill Harrison and Bill Lynch, who contributed fine articles on the development of set dancing outside Ireland. I also wish to thank the staff of Cecil Sharp House in London for their help and hospitality when I visited their wonderful library to research the quadrilles. Particular thanks to Diana Jewitt, who helped me so much there.

INTRODUCTION

Since the publication of *Toss the Feathers* in 1995, the Irish set-dancing revival has continued and many more fine sets have been recovered. Some of the dances included here are old traditional sets, while a few 'new' sets, though not traditional dances, have been put together and have become popular in different places.

My fascination with quadrille-based dances from other countries and their obvious similarities to our own sets led me to include here some set dances from Canada, America and Australia. I am indebted to Elizabeth MacDonald, Pete Brett and Jean Ver Hoeven for sharing their dances and expert knowledge of these sets with me. I believe these dances will be of particular interest to dancers and to students of dance history. Elizabeth is currently collecting traditional dances from the Maritime Provinces in Canada and will publish them at a future date.

Three waltz dances are included here too. The Truro Waltz Quadrilles has been danced for generations in Nova Scotia, while the Royal Cotillion has previously been published in older dance manuals. It is similar in style to the popular Waltz Cotillion, included in *Toss the Feathers*. The Pride of Erin Waltz, although neither a cotillion nor a quadrille, is a beautiful dance which I deem worthy of inclusion here. Slight variations of it are danced regularly in Scotland and Northern Ireland and occasionally in the rest of Ireland.

HISTORY

Irish set dancing evolved from French court dancing. In tracing the development of set dancing, I have examined some historical factors that have influenced its evolution. A more detailed history of set dancing is included in my first set-dance book, *Toss the Feathers*.

Some of the earliest references to dancing, together with the dances, their European counterparts and the conflicts – historical, political and religious – that affected them are mentioned. We look at the eighteenth- and nineteenth-century Irish dance masters, who combined European dances and Irish music and dance steps to create round country dances and later set dances.

Events in the twentieth century, particularly in the 1930s, that led to the decline of house dances and had an extremely adverse effect on set dancing are discussed. The cotillions and quadrilles – the original dances that came from France and were taken on board by the dance masters – are introduced. Finally we take a general look at some aspects of the modern set-dancing revival and where it stands today. In developing this area, I am indebted to Elizabeth MacDonald, Bill Harrison and Bill Lynch for their excellent articles on the development of set dancing outside Ireland.

THE SETS

The second part of this book contains a list of the sets I have learned in the past five years from various sources. Some sets were given to me by local people in the areas where they originate, while others were shared with me by dancers and dancing teachers in various places. I am extremely grateful to all those who so generously and patiently shared their time and knowledge with me. I have tried to record the dances as accurately as possible and I accept responsibility for any errors included here. I am aware that there are also other, equally valid versions of some of these sets. The instructions I have given here for the sets are mostly standardised, so that they can be more easily understood – my wish is that people will take the time to dance and enjoy them and, if possible, visit their places of origin. I use the terms 'gent' and 'lady' when referring to the dancers, as this is the accepted terminology for set dancing.

COMMON SET-DANCING MOVEMENTS

LEAD AROUND
1. Each couple face anticlockwise in the set, gents on the inside. They take crossed hands in front and right hands on top and dance anticlockwise around the set without turning (8 bars).
2. With each gent's right arm around his partner's waist and her left hand on his shoulder, all couples dance anticlockwise around the set without turning (8 bars).

HOUSE
1. Partners take waltz hold and dance anticlockwise around the set, turning clockwise four times (to each position) as they dance around (8 bars).
2. Partners take crossed hands facing each other and dance anticlockwise around the set, turning clockwise (usually) as they dance (8 bars).

HOME (DANCE IN PLACE)

In waltz hold, couples dance in their own place, turning clockwise twice (8 bars).

SQUARE

1. In waltz hold, all couples slide (1 2 3, kick) to the position on the right, turn slightly clockwise, slide, starting on the other foot, to the opposite position (1 2, 1 2 3), then dance anticlockwise back to place, turning clockwise twice. Sometimes, instead of the dancers turning during the last four bars, the slide movement is danced all the way around (8 bars).

2. In waltz hold, couples dance 'sevens' across to opposite positions – gents passing back to back – turn slightly clockwise and dance 'sevens' through opposite position – ladies passing back to back – turn slightly clockwise again and repeat both movements back to place (8 bars). (Sometimes this movement, with the same steps, is danced to each position, instead of across the set in a square. When this is done, it is called a diamond).

3. In waltz hold, all couples slide (1 2 3, lift or kick) to the position on the right, dance on the spot there, turning clockwise slightly (1 2 3, 1 2 3), so that their backs are to the opposite position, reverse with slide step (1 2 3, lift or kick) to the opposite position, dance on the spot there, turning clockwise slightly (1 2 3, 1 2 3) to face towards the third position, and repeat all the movements, dancing forward to the next position and reversing back to home (16 bars).

BODY

Partners take each other in waltz hold. All couples dance one step into the centre and one step back (2 bars), then turn clockwise into the position on the right (2 bars). They repeat the movements three times, dancing anticlockwise around the set to their own places (12 bars). This is the most commonly danced body in set dancing. It is danced in many sets from Cork, Kerry and Clare and in both polkas and hornpipes (16 bars).

SET-DANCING STEPS

A wide variety of set-dancing steps are incorporated in local dancing styles. To learn these steps properly, dancers should study the style and steps of older traditional dancers in the areas where the sets originate, or, if this is not possible, they should learn them from a competent dancing instructor.

Nowadays many of the popular sets are danced in a uniform style which in some cases bears little resemblance to the traditional form of the set. While a certain degree of uniformity is probably inevitable, we must at all times endeavour to preserve the unique style and steps of the various sets. The extra effort required to assimilate the individual traits that give each set its character and appeal will be well rewarded. Indeed, it is necessary to do this in order to enjoy different sets. All of the dances are special – like the people who developed them and danced them locally for generations.

Keeping this in mind, I believe it best to describe here only the standard basic steps for each musical form; it is practically impossible to describe in written form – or indeed to learn from a book – the intricacies and visual effect of the more traditional steps. One has to see them to understand and learn them properly.

There are two basic steps from which most of the others are created: polka steps and reel steps.

POLKA STEPS

Gents start on the left foot, dancing left right left (L R L). Ladies start on the right foot, dancing R L R. The weight is transferred on the first step and kept mainly on that side during the three steps that are danced in one bar of music. The weight is then transferred back to the other side on the first step of the next three and kept on that side during the next bar of music. This sequence is continued throughout the set.

Gent: L R L	R L R	L R L
Lady: R L R	L R L	R L R

In some sets the following steps are danced when advancing and retiring:

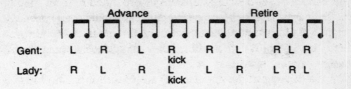

	Advance				Retire			
Gent:	L	R	L	R kick	R	L	R	L R
Lady:	R	L	R	L kick	L	R	L	R L

REEL STEPS

The reel step used in most movements consists of a four-part sequence.

FOR GENTS

1. Start by transferring the weight from the ball of the right foot to the heel. (This is almost, but not quite, a gentle hop on the heel.)
2. Step onto the left foot, transferring the weight to the left at the same time. The weight stays on the left side for the rest of the sequence.
3. Now step onto the right foot again, keeping the weight on the left.
4. Complete the sequence by stepping back onto the left foot.

FOR LADIES

1. Start by transferring the weight from the ball of the left foot to the heel. (This is almost, but not quite, a gentle hop on the heel.)
2. Step onto the right foot, transferring the weight to the right at the same time. The weight stays on the right side for the rest of the sequence.
3. Now step onto the left foot again, keeping the weight on the right.
4. Complete the sequence by stepping back onto the right foot.

These steps are danced in one bar of music. Ladies and gents start the next sequence of steps on their other foot. Note that (h) means coming down on the heel.

Different steps are danced in most sets when advancing and retiring. The following sequence of steps is danced when advancing, in two bars of music:

FOR GENTS
1. Start by transferring the weight from the ball of the right foot to the heel, as in the other sequence. Step forward onto the left foot, transferring the weight to the left.
2. Repeat Step 1, starting on the left foot and stepping forward, transferring the weight to the right side.
3. Repeat Step 1 again, starting on the right foot and stepping onto the left.
4. Step onto the right foot, keeping the weight on the left side.
5. Finally, step onto the left foot again to complete the advance.

FOR LADIES
1. Transfer the weight from the ball of the left foot to the heel, as in the other sequence. Step forward onto the right foot, transferring the weight to the right side.
2. Repeat Step 1, starting on the right foot and stepping forward, transferring the weight to the left side.
3. Repeat Step 1 again, starting on the left foot and stepping onto the right.
4. Step onto the left foot, keeping the weight on the right side.
5. Finally, step onto the right foot again to complete the advance.

ADVANCE (REEL)

| Gent: | R h | L | L h | R | R h | L | R | L | L h |
| Lady: | L h | R | R h | L | L h | R | L | R | R h |

When retiring, the same sequence is danced, starting on the other foot and dancing backward instead of forward on the first three steps.

RETIRE (REEL)

| Gent: | L h | R | R h | L | L h | R | L | R | R h |
| Lady: | R h | L | L h | R | R h | L | R | L | L h |

HORNPIPE STEPS

Steps danced in the hornpipe figures are similar to those described here for the reel, though obviously danced at a slower speed. The movement transferring the weight from the ball of the foot to the heel of the same foot (1) is usually a more emphasised 'hop' when dancing to a hornpipe.

JIG STEPS

Jig figures can vary from set to set: they are danced to the steps described for the polka in some sets and to the steps described for the reel in others.

JIG STEP ('POLKA' OR 'DOWN' VERSION (- 1 2 3))

Gent: L   R L   R   L R
Lady: R   L R   L   R L

JIG STEP ('REEL' VERSION (HOP 1 2 3))

Gent: R   L   R L   L   R   L R   R
         h   h   h
Lady: L   R   L R   R   L   R L   R
         h   h   h

JIG STEP ADVANCE ('POLKA' VERSION)

Gent: R   L   R   L   R
         h   kick, or lift foot
Lady: L   R   L   R   L
         h   kick, or lift foot

JIG STEP RETIRE ('POLKA' VERSION)

Gent: L   R   L   R L R
         h
Lady: R   L   R   L R L
         h

14

Jig Step Advance ('Reel' Version)

Gent:	R	L	L	R	R	L	R	L
	h		h		h			
Lady:	L	R	R	L	L	R	L	R
	h		h		h			

Jig Step Retire ('Reel' Version)

Gent:	L	R	R	L	L	R	L	R
	h		h		h			
Lady:	R	L	L	R	R	L	R	L
	h		h		h			

A HISTORY OF SET DANCING

EARLY IRISH DANCING

The earliest reference to dancing in Irish literature recalls a visit by the Mayor of Waterford to O'Driscoll of Baltimore in 1413, where carolling is said to have taken place.[1] Carolling was a processional combination of singing that was popular in Normandy at the time the Normans first came to Ireland – in 1169 – so it is quite likely that they were responsible for its introduction here.

The three dances mentioned in Irish records are the hay or hey, the *rinnce fada* and the trenchmore, sometimes called the *rinnce mór*. Hay probably comes from 'haie', a French word for a row of stakes in a fence. It was used to refer to a line of soldiers or dancers. The *rinnce fada* is mentioned many times over the next century. A wild processional dance, it was quite likely related to the surviving fading or furry dance of Cornwall. The trenchmore was also mentioned frequently by many dance historians. It was published by John Playford in 1651 as a 'long dance for as many as will'.

Dancing seems to have been widespread in Ireland from the middle of the seventeenth century. In his *Voyage through the Kingdom of Ireland* (1681), Thomas Dinnely described the Irish as being addicted to dancing – 'after their country fashion, that is, the long dance, one after another of all conditions, masters, mistresses and servants'.

Towards the end of the seventeenth century, John Dunton wrote that 'on Sundays and Holydays, all the people resorted with the piper to the village green, where the young folk dance till the cows come home. There was no occasion from which dancing was absent'.

EUROPEAN INFLUENCES

The origins of set dancing can be traced back to the dancing which developed at the academy at the court of King Louis XIV of France (1638–1715), the Sun King. In Louis's centralised court system, the prominent nobles of the day were, for political reasons, prevailed upon to spend much of their time at court; because they had so much free time, dancing and other leisure pastimes were important. Professional dancing masters were employed in the Academie de Danse, which was founded by the king and run by Charles de

Beauchamp. Its job was continually to create and teach new dances for the amusement of the nobles. In their search for new dances, Louis's dancing masters travelled the country learning the peasant dances, which they then adapted into court dances.

One of the most enduring of the dances they discovered was the *branle*. There were many localised versions of the *branle*, which is believed to be the forerunner of the later cotillions and quadrilles, from which our sets developed.

IRISH DANCING MASTERS

Irish dancing masters of the eighteenth and nineteenth centuries were aware of and influenced by French dancing, etiquette, manners and deportment. Surviving information about them describing their own dress and mannerisms shows how proud they were of this 'European connection'. Indeed, they were known to teach not only dancing but also social etiquette and fencing – the latter activities surely being more associated with royal courts and the upper classes than with Irish peasant society.

English society was itself strongly affected by developments at the French courts at this time; the English landowning classes and military personnel in Ireland brought French dances and associated activities here, where they were adopted by the Irish dancing masters and passed on by them to their pupils. The dancing masters taught the families of all classes, so it was in their own interest to be aware of and to be able to teach the fashionable dances of the day.

In an article written by Maurice Lenihan and first published in 1867,[2] there are descriptions of three types of dancing masters that existed at that time. Those at the top of their profession, described as 'slightly ridiculous and pretentious' men, gallicised their names, claimed to have been trained in France and aped the manners and dress of their upper-class clients. At the bottom were those described as 'village hop merchants', who taught the basic simple steps required for the crossroads dance. In between was the dance master who taught all classes. He was the person responsible for bringing the cotillions and quadrilles from the big houses to the crossroads, where they thrived as vigorous social dances accompanied by the music of the people and evolved into both early figure or country dances and country set dances as we know them today.

The dancing masters thus came to prominence in the eighteenth century, although they may have been around long before then. They created the steps for solo dances, as well as steps and figure movements for round or figure dances, and later for sets, using as their source the movements of the imported cotillions and quadrilles.

The first traveller's account of the dancing masters is by Arthur Young (1741–1820), who was in Ireland between 1776 and 1779. He informs us in *A Tour in Ireland* that 'dance masters of their own rank travel through the country from cabin to cabin with a piper or blind fiddler. Their pay is sixpence a quarter.' He goes on to say, 'Besides the Irish Jig, which they can dance with a most luxuriant expression, Minuets and Country Dances are taught and I even heard some talk of Cotillions coming in.' The French cotillions were in England in 1770.

In literature, the dancing master is treated with affection or sometimes condescension. Described by Young as 'whimsical, shabby, genteel in dress, grandiloquent in speech', he is later said to have been dignified, with good carriage and deportment and, as a gentleman, always to have endeavoured to instil into his more promising pupils something of this spirit. He was usually accommodated in some farmer's house in each district in which he was teaching, using the kitchen or barn as his salon, sometimes sharing it with the hedge schoolmaster. In return, he taught dancing – including the dances 'in vogue in fashionable circles' – and deportment to the farmer's children. This indicates that he adopted and taught society dances to all classes of people.

His methods were to teach basic steps first and then the dance. When he did not have the correct steps, or his pupils were not talented enough to assimilate them, he taught his own steps – more than likely ones that were already familiar to his pupils. The steps would reflect the rhythms of the music with which the pupils were familiar; in this way our sets developed differently in different parts of Ireland.

The Irish dancing masters thus adapted foreign dances, using their own talents and knowledge to combine the varied, intricate movements of the new cotillions (of the eighteenth century) and quadrilles (of the nineteenth century) with their own lively steps to create round country or *céilí* dances and the various sets we dance today.

THE GAELIC LEAGUE

The Gaelic League was founded in 1893, with the stated objective of 'recreating a separate cultural Irish nation'. They believed that, in order to achieve this, a process of what Douglas Hyde called de-Anglicisation was necessary. This process entailed refusing to imitate the English in their language, literature, music, games, dress or ideas. The league's primary aim was to keep the Irish language alive; they later turned their attention to other aspects of Irish culture, including dancing. Misguidedly, they banned their members from taking part in all the old traditional dances that survived at the time – round and country dances as well as quadrilles.

According to Francis Roche,[3] 'It was unfortunate that the work of our old national dances should have largely fallen to the lot of those who were poorly equipped for the task. For the most part, they were lacking in insight and a pure appreciation of the pure old style and had, it appears, but a slender knowledge of the old repertoire.'

It was rather ironic that the first public *céilí* ever held was in London's Bloomsbury Hall in 1897. The event was organised by Fionán MacColum, the Scottish Secretary of the Gaelic League in London, who said that the dances performed on the occasion included 'Sets, Quadrilles and Waltzes to Irish music'.

Some years later, members of the Gaelic League Dancing Commission, which was formed in 1929, resurrected many of the dances that had disappeared, and other dances were composed to replace those that had vanished. As a result, there is now a good variety of *céilí* dances available. In spite of the ban, set dances, with their informal style, survived in all dancing areas, even in the Gaeltacht areas of Munster.

DANCING AND RELIGION

From the earliest times, in almost all civilisations and societies, the relationship between religious authorities and dancing has been less than harmonious. This has been true from the time of the Old Testament, through the early Christian period and medieval times, up to the first half of the twentieth century.

In Ireland, the church authorities always seemed to view dancing as 'lewd, licentious, immoral and unbecoming to its flock'. There are many instances from the seventeenth century onwards, documented by Breandán Breathnach in *Dancing in Ireland*, where dancing was condemned – as were the unfortunate pipers who were largely, it would seem, held responsible for its popularity.

One of the reasons given for the church's view of dancing was the association which existed at wakes, festivals, patterns and Sunday-afternoon gatherings between music, dancing and drink – with the resulting improper behaviour. Ladies were particularly likely to be denounced if they were known to favour dancing. Many bishops – Dr Plunkett of Meath (1790–1819), Dr Bray of Cashel and Emly (1746) and Dr Moylan of Kerry (1785) – condemned dance gatherings in their dioceses and threatened punishments, up to excommunication, on those who dared to disobey them.

Similar attitudes and instances are related from the 1930s. There are numerous instances listed of musicians, who were held responsible for the dancing, being physically assaulted and their instruments being broken or destroyed. One such victim, a piper named Stephen Ruane, from Galway, was forced to abandon his livelihood as a professional musician; with no alternative way of surviving, he ended his days in the Galway workhouse.

Francis O'Neill declared that 'no defensible reason, other than the defence of morality, had ever been assigned for the hostility of Irish clergy to music and dancing'. This he found hard to justify, taking into consideration that the activities thus condemned were conducted publicly – in houses, in fields or at crossroads and among families, friends and neighbours.

As commercial dance halls became popular, a clamour was raised for them to be controlled by the state. An article in the *Irish Times* in 1929 claimed that 'The clergy, judges and police were all in agreement concerning the baneful effect of drink and low dance halls. Further restrictions on the sale of drink, strict supervision of dance halls [and] the banning of all-night dances would abolish many inducements to sexual vice, but what was needed above all was recognition of the fact that the nation's proudest and most precious heritage was slipping from its grasp.'

This drive to establish state control of dancing was realised with the passing of the Public Dance Halls Act of 1935, which required all public dances to be licensed and laid down the conditions under which licences might be issued by the district justices. This piece of legislation was 'An act to make provision for the licensing, control and supervision of places used for public dancing, and to make provision for other matters connected with the matters aforesaid.'

The provisions of the act were very restrictive with regard to the conditions under which a licence to hold a dance could be obtained.

This, combined with the fact that the civic guards and local clergy applied them to house dances as well as public-dance-hall dances, made it difficult for those who had held house dances to keep them going – and in the end effectively put an end to them. In this way, a wonderful social aspect of life in rural Ireland was gradually brought to a sad end.

At the time, the country-house dances were already under pressure from public dance halls. Although it would have seemed logical to preserve them as a real alternative to the public dances, they were instead penalised out of existence under the legislation. There are few possible justifications for the hostile attitude of both church and civil authorities towards what was essentially a harmless pastime.

SET DANCING

The origins of set dancing can be traced back to the French cotillion, which was first mentioned in Ireland by Arthur Young. A French *contredanse*, it was claimed that it had been developed from or inspired by English country dancing of the time.

Cecil Sharp, one of the foremost English dance historians and perhaps the person most responsible for reviving English country dancing, wrote that, when confronted by the rising popularity of English dances in France, the French started to appreciate and revive their own country dances. The cotillion is one of the best-documented of these French dances. It was known in France in 1723, in Germany in 1741 and in England in 1770.

When dancing the cotillion, four couples started in square formation. They danced a procession or lead around in the entrée and a figure during the refrain, or second period of music, finishing back in their own positions each time. The figures that were danced had movements that were also found in the quadrilles and are present in our sets today. They included:

(a) *les ronds* – circular movements to left or right,
(b) *la grande chaîne* – chain all round, gents to the right, ladies to the left, and
(c) *les moulinets* – hands in the centre and dance around (star).

It is said by Curt Sachs[4] that the constant repetition of entrée and refrain became boring, leading to a decline in the popularity of the cotillion. In the early nineteenth century this dance was reconstructed to include a larger variety of figures, including waltzes and social games involving flirting and forfeits, as well as selected parts of old circular dances. The cotillion degenerated as a result of this search for endless variety and eventually all but disappeared. In the early nineteenth century, however, another dance form, developed from the early cotillion, gained popularity. This was the quadrille, which has survived in many forms down to the present day.

The French word 'quadrille' is derived from the Italian 'quadriglia', meaning a troop of horsemen who formed a square when taking part in a military display or tournament. In the time of Napoleon, a popular *contredanse* – which was usually danced in sets of four, five or six figures, several of which were complicated – was developed from this. The quadrilles arrived in England, Scotland and Ireland around 1816. They are believed to have been brought to most European countries by military personnel, diplomats and other travellers of the time. They became the most popular dances of the day, perhaps because of the variety of movement they offered.

The first quadrilles had intricate steps that were described using terms developed by French dancing masters and nowadays associated with ballroom dancing – French terms such as *jeté*, *chassé*, *assemblé*, *balancé* and *changement de jambe*. With the passing of time, while the movements survived the steps gradually disappeared – with the exception of the easy walking step known as the *pas marché*.

Like most popular social dances of the time, the quadrilles were first danced by the upper classes but spread rapidly among the ordinary people in all countries. They were learned by the dancing masters of the time and eventually changed by them into localised forms. Here in Ireland, the dancing masters taught the dances to their local music, using appropriate steps already known to, or composed by, the dancing master. According to Flett & Flett in *Scottish Traditional Dancing* (1964), the dancers or the MC at social dances selected the figures to be danced from the large selection that was available.

An interesting social development of the day was the introduction of little dance books which ladies carried in their purses to the ballroom. These were tiny, ornate and sometimes exquisitely bound little books, some finished in the finest leather, which contained a concise description of a quadrille figure on each page. When, at the beginning of a set, the MC called the numbers of the quadrilles to be danced, the ladies looked up the figures in their little books and were thus made aware of the movements that were required. An extremely interesting collection of these delightful little books is preserved today in Cecil Sharp House in London. The practice of using call-cards continues in many forms of social dancing, including our set dances, to this day.

As time went on, certain combinations of quadrille figures gained in popularity and became fixed into sets of quadrilles, so that by the middle of the nineteenth century there were believed to be around a dozen sets of quadrilles that were popularly danced. As time went by, however, many of these sets disappeared; eventually the only surviving old quadrille sets were:

(a) the First Set of Quadrilles, which was known as the Quadrilles,
(b) the Lancer Quadrilles and
(c) the Caledonian Quadrilles.

The First Set of Quadrilles became the most popular set with dancers in Paris at the beginning of the nineteenth century. In London it is said to have become known as the Payne set, taking its name from a dancing teacher and writer called Payne, who, interestingly, was said to be a woman.

The second set of quadrilles to become popular among nineteenth-century dancers was *les lanciers* – 'the lancers'. The origin of this set has been claimed by various sources. One of the most eminent dance historians, Curt Sachs, writes in *World History of the Dance* (1937) that the set was composed by a French dancing master named Duval at the request of a lancer regiment based in Dublin in 1817. Another source argues that it was created at Fontainebleau as a commission for a French regiment. Whatever its origin, its movements are said to reflect the various drills and formations familiar to the military. *Les Lanciers: A Second Set of Quadrilles for the Piano Forte* (1820), by a dancing teacher named Hart, describes how the lancers was danced in good society in the summer of 1819.

The third set of quadrilles that was to be enduringly popular was the Caledonian Quadrilles. It is mentioned by Scottish sources and would appear to have its origins in – or at least to have got its name from – that country. It is also described in dancing manuals dating from the end of the nineteenth century.

Many of the movements described in these quadrille figures by

Edward Scott in *Dancing as an Art and Pastime* (1892) and by others are found in the sets we dance today:

- *allemande* – Turn the lady under the arm or link arms.
- *avant* – Advance.
- *balancé* – Set to your partner – when facing each other, dance slide steps to the right and back to the left. This was also done with the person on the other side. Another meaning of 'balancé', when dancing in line, was 'stepping from side to side'.
- *chaîne anglaise* – The right and left, which is the square danced in the first figure of the Clare Lancers. There are other versions of it in other sets.
- *chaîne des dames* – Ladies' chain.
- *chassé croisé* – Partners pass each other sideways, the gent passing behind the lady. This movement is like the sidestep used in many sets and *céilí* dances.
- *les grâces* – Fairly similar to the High Gates in various sets and to Contrary in the Orange and Green Set.
- *moulinet* – A Turnstile, similar to the star or hands in the centre.
- *promenade* – Lead around.

The Modern Set-Dancing Revival

While the Public Dance Halls Act of 1935 put an end to most of them, the house dances survived to some degree in a number of more traditional places. It is fair to say that the dance-halls act and its rigorous enforcement was not the only reason the sets declined. The growing influence of the media, which brought imported music, dances and ideas to Ireland, greatly influenced people, particularly the younger generation. Increased mobility gave access to various kinds of social gatherings and entertainment that were perhaps more appealing to the young. Another major factor in the decline of house dances was the waves of emigration which in many remote, traditional areas removed the greater part of a generation from their communities and cultural influences and thus broke the continuity of the dances.

In the 1930s and 1940s the local halls catered mostly for *céilí* dancing, but sets that were indigenous to the area sometimes survived.

In the 1940s, 1950s and even the 1960s, house and crossroad dances continued to be held, too, usually on special family, religious or other festive occasions. Threshing dances, for example, were held in the autumn each year.

In this way, the Caledonian Set in Clare, the Castle or Cashel Set in Tipperary and many sets in Kerry and Cork continued to be danced, sometimes even as part of the evening's entertainment in the halls. It has been said that, even though the *céilí* dances were held to be more Irish than sets by the authorities, the only dances that could be seen in the Kerry Gaeltacht were sets.

Other sets which had flourished in the 1930s, such as the Labasheeda Reel Set, the Lancers, the Orange and Green and the Paris Set in Clare, went into decline, however, and, were it not for the dedication and interest of the old-time music and dancing teachers, they might never have been revived. The work done by these men and women and by other, later enthusiasts ensured that Ireland now has possibly the richest store of traditional sets ever. Moreover, the founding of Comhaltas Ceoltóirí Éireann in 1951 led to a strong renewal of interest in traditional Irish music. In the wake of this renewed interest, the dancing also revived. People danced both *céilí* dances and set dances at *fleadhanna* and *céilithe*.

The revival of set dancing benefited greatly from the series of competitions organised by the Gaelic Athletic Association and Comhaltas Ceoltóirí Éireann in the 1970s. Teams of set dancers from various parts of the country took part in these competitions, thus showing their own sets and style of dancing to everybody.

Perhaps the person who did most to inspire the revival of set dancing in the 1980s and 1990s was the late Connie Ryan, a Tipperary man who, through his set-dancing workshops, brought this type of dance to every corner of Ireland and indeed far beyond. Connie's workshop weekends usually consisted of an informal evening's entertainment on the Friday and a full day of teaching on Saturday followed by a Saturday-night set-dancing *céilí*, a Sunday-morning class and a Sunday-afternoon *céilí*. The sets he taught were always danced at the *céilithe*, along with other popular sets.

Connie was born and reared near Clonoulty, a village between Thurles and Cashel in County Tipperary. He often spoke of the dances that were held regularly in his own home there in his youth. It was there that he developed his love of dancing and probably heard some of the colourful expressions, used by local characters, that he used from time to time during his dancing career. He often mentioned the crossroad dances held in neighbouring parishes when he was young. One of the locations he mentioned, in Ballyboy, Upperchurch, was familiar to me as it was located close to my own home; indeed my father sometimes played music for the dancing there.

Connie initially taught *céilí* and set dancing in Dublin and later around Ireland as a member of the Coiste Rince, or Dancing Committee of Comhaltas Ceoltóirí Éireann. In later years he branched out on his own and specialised in teaching the sets. Many of these sets were revived during the 1970s, when competition set dancing became popular and seeing these competitions made people realise the value of this aspect of their culture. They were encouraged to search out and revive their own local sets, and Connie spent much of his time searching out, learning and teaching many of these sets. He travelled throughout Ireland and later taught sets in many European countries as well as in many places in the eastern United States.

Connie taught dancing for well over thirty years, until his untimely death in 1997. His passing – after a long illness, which did not however stop him from dancing or teaching – was a very sad occasion for his family and his legions of pupils, fans and friends around the world. He has left a wonderful legacy of set dancing to us: his sheer drive, enthusiasm and obvious love of dancing inspired set-dancing people everywhere.

The other major influence on the set-dancing revival was the development of the Willie Clancy Summer School in Milltown Malbay, County Clare. One of the principal organisers of this summer school was Muiris Ó Rócháin, a native of Kerry and a teacher in Spanish Point, a short distance from Milltown. The first summer school took place in Milltown in August 1973. The initial focus of the school was music and in particular pipe music.

In 1982 Cork dancing teacher Joe O'Donovan, who had been teaching workshops in various places around Ireland for many years, was invited to teach a set-dancing class in conjunction with the music classes. Joe is one of our best-loved and most respected dancing teachers. With his wife Siobhán, he has travelled and taught extensively – in the United States and Europe as well as in every part of Ireland.

Joe's set classes in Milltown were extremely successful and many of his pupils went home to teach the dances that they had learned to their own friends and other enthusiasts. Many of the well-known teachers and dancers of today began their own dancing careers in this way. One of the most influential of those early dancers was Terry Moylan, who with his friends formed Brooks Academy, the set-dancing section of the Pipers' Club in Dublin. Brooks Academy has done marvellous work in popularising the revived dances through dance publications by Terry Moylan and Eileen O'Doherty and their music recordings, weekly classes and various workshops.

In the Willie Clancy Summer School, emphasis was placed on preserving the old styles of dancing, be they from the local areas of west Clare or from other parts of Ireland. West Clare dancing was always highly regarded because of the beautiful, spectacular 'battering' style of dancing displayed in many of the wonderful sets from around Milltown, Mullagh and Quilty. Through attending the classes here, dancers from everywhere came to know, love and respect the old-style dancers and their beautiful steps and styles. People like the late Dan Furey, who had been teaching dancing throughout west Clare for much of his life, and his friend James Keane became icons wherever Clare sets were danced. Another famous Clare dancer was the late Willie Keane, who was regarded by many as one of the finest battering-style dancers they had ever seen. Indeed, many of our present-day battering-style dancers attempt to emulate Willie's wonderful dancing.

Milltown Malbay has gone from strength to strength over the years and is now the largest dancing summer school of all, with many thousands of people having visited it since it began. The school is held in the first week of July each year and has a variety of teachers there for its duration.

Other summer festivals carried on the tradition. Set dancing developed at the South Sligo Summer School in Tubbercurry under the guidance of Connie Ryan, who also taught for its first two years at the Joe Mooney Summer School in Drumshanbo, County Leitrim, where I have been teaching for a number of years. These and other schools continue to grow in popularity, so that now it is possible to dance the summer through, should one wish to do so.

Set dancing is now well established in all the major towns and cities in Ireland. Sets were always danced in the rural areas, but it is only since the set-dancing revival in the 1970s that the urban population has been involved in this kind of dancing as much as it is now. The presence of set-dance callers at the popular set-dance nights enables anybody with a reasonable knowledge of the sets to take part in the evening's activities and dance different sets that he or she does not know particularly well. Some people disapprove of calling and prefer to dance a certain central repertoire of sets that their patrons eventually memorise.

Although everyone would agree that the most popular sets should not be called to any great extent, calling is vital to the survival of many beautiful sets. In the absence of a capable caller, the only occasion on which people can dance different sets is at a workshop *céilí*, where the visiting teacher will usually call some of the sets that have been taught during the day's class.

What makes the sets of today unique is the variety of steps and dancing styles that they contain; these steps and styles have evolved with the passing years. This gives the sets their enduring popularity with so many people. It is vitally important that we make every effort to preserve the various styles as accurately as possible, otherwise the sets will gradually lose their colour and individuality and eventually disappear, with only the best-known remaining.

As people travel more and learn many different sets, there is a tendency to dance all sets in the style a person prefers, regardless of the fact that a particular set has traditionally been danced in a different – perhaps slower or less noisy and less flamboyant – style. Although it is uplifting to see and appreciate the great dancers we see from time to time, we should remember that if everyone danced in the same style the rest would not long survive. While keeping in mind that dance is a social pastime and that we dance for recreation and fun, it is surely important that we respect tradition and try to preserve the integrity and original local style of the sets.

One of the recurring comments in dance histories since the sixteenth century is the complaint that dancing has become too wild and fast, losing its quality in the process. It would appear that all ages of dancing had this problem, and today's set dancing is no exception. Significantly, in the more traditional dancing areas, such as Clare, the music is usually played at a slower, more suitable pace and the intricate steps that are so admired by all dancers continue to be danced there. We can only hope that more people will come to understand and appreciate the music and realise that speed is a hindrance to the enjoyment of both the music and the sets.

Set dancing flourishes in many places outside Ireland too. It is taught at numerous festivals, summer schools and other major events, particularly in Britain and the United States, as well as in various

European countries. These countries now have their own expert teachers, some of whom attend the various summer schools and weekend workshops in Ireland. Many of them are visited from time to time by Irish teachers and dancers. It would appear that language barriers do not exist where set dancing is concerned.

Perhaps the first place to be affected by the set-dancing revival was Britain, where Irish cultural activities such as music, dance and Gaelic games had flourished in the country's many Irish communities and Irish centres. Set dancing is particularly strong in the London area, where it has for many years benefited from the expertise and dedication of numerous fine teachers such as Geoff Holland and Michael Keane.

On a recent visit to London, Bill Lynch, the editor of the popular *Set Dancing News* – and a man who has himself made a major contribution to the set-dancing revival with his excellent Set Dancing Web site and his magazine – spoke to both Michael and Geoff about their experiences. Bill has kindly contributed the following article:

IRISH SET DANCING IN LONDON

Until the 1980s the only set dancing in London occurred occasionally in pubs at weddings and other gatherings. *Céilí* dancing was very popular before the set-dancing revival, with several long-running weekly live music *céilís* across greater London. London was probably unequalled in *céilí* dancing at the time. The full repertoire of *céilí* dances was danced without calling. The acceptance of set dancing made slow progress throughout the 1908s due to the strong *céilí*-dancing scene.

Comhaltas began promoting set dancing in the early 1980s by organising exhibitions with dancers from Ireland and competitions for dancers from across England. Sets were also danced regularly at monthly Comhaltas music sessions. In 1983 Michael Keane taught a class twice a month in Hammersmith for Comhaltas. From 1985 he started teaching independently in several venues across north London. He was involved with the Haringey Irish Centre from 1986 and still teaches there today, as well as in Tooting and Kilburn.

Other influential teachers in London were Sarah Monaghan (Sorcha Ní Mhuineacháin), Geoff Holland and Kevin McMahon. Sarah taught in Camden from 1984, and that class has continued with Geoff since 1989. He also teaches a thriving set-dancing class in Cecil Sharp House, the home of

English folk dancing. Kevin taught very popular classes at Áras na nGael in Kilburn from 1990 and organised regular live-music *céilís* there.

The first set-dancing *céilí* was held in August 1985 at the London Irish Centre in Camden. Five sets were danced that evening, as well as *céilí* dances. Set-dancing *céilís* were also held informally in Haringey before the centre's official opening, in October 1987, and continued there every Sunday for many years. There was also live-music set dancing in Camden on Sunday evenings, in competition with the long-running live-music *céilí* dancing in an adjacent hall. The most enduring and popular set-dance *céilí* in London is Geoff Holland's session, held on the afternoon of the first Sunday of each month in Camden.

The first sets taught in London included the Caledonian, South Kerry, Ballyvourney Jig, North Kerry, Auban, Sliabh Luachra and South Galway Sets. Joe O'Donovan taught the first workshop in London in 1983 or 1984, when he introduced the Lancers, Cashel and Mazurka Sets. The Plain Set was introduced by Connie Ryan at his first workshop in November 1989, organised by Kevin McMahon. Connie returned to London every year until his death in 1997. Other teachers visiting London include Terry Moylan, Pat Moroney, Martin and Francis Bolger, Larry Lynch, Mick Mulkerrin, Pat Murphy and Timmy McCarthy.

There has always been good cooperation between teachers and classes in London. Event leaflets are available in most classes and events are announced even if they compete with other ones. Since 1994 Geoff Holland has published *The London Set Dancing Diary*, which lists events across London and is widely read. Teachers have always freely shared sets with each other and been keen to introduce sets learned at workshops and in Ireland. The repertoire of sets is very large – Geoff Holland once counted 48 different sets danced in his Camden class in a year. There is no hesitation to fill the floor when an unusual dance is called at a *céilí*. The London crowd are excellent dancers and are frequently seen at events across Ireland.

One of the greatest festivals of music and dance anywhere is the North American Comhaltas Convention, which is hosted by Comhaltas branches in a different North American city each year. Various Irish set-dance teachers have attended and taught at the convention over the years. Many of the dancers who attend the event teach their own classes in various places throughout North America, and the dances continue to spread and flourish there. In many cases, the teachers do not have any connection with Ireland other than a love of the dances. Although sets are danced across the United States, they are more established in the areas traditionally associated with the Irish – places such as New York, Boston, Washington, Philadelphia and Chicago.

The following information on the background and development of set dancing in the New York area was supplied by Bill Harrison, a resident of Manhattan. Bill is a fine dancer and a regular visitor to dancing festivals in Ireland.

IRISH SET DANCING IN NEW YORK

Prior to the revival of interest in set dancing, social Irish dancing in New York meant *céilí* dancing. This situation had persisted from early in the century through the late 1970s, and the *céilís* in New York run by the Gaelic League or the Irish Arts Centre were opportunities to dance a greater variety of *céilí* dances than even today. Sets were danced occasionally, but generally in private clubs or county organisations like the Doonbeg Club or the Clare Association, where the sets danced were the local ones, like the Caledonian or Plain Set, which were familiar to the members.

In the late 1970s and into the early 1980s, the traditional-music revival was beginning to spark a wider interest in dancing the sets. In Ireland, 1982 saw the appearance of the first workshops on sets among the music workshops at the Willie Clancy Week festival, and the Pipers' Club began to give workshops. And this revival in Ireland began to spark interest among some of the dancers on this side of the water.

When visiting Ireland, dancers from New York began to see the sets that were emerging in Ireland. And at sessions like the Irish Arts Centre's popular Monday-night sessions, or at summer classes in the Catskill mountains, people would watch dancers from clubs like Doonbeg doing this odd, flat, not-like-the-*céilí* footwork that came to be called, for a while, the 'Catskill shuffle'. (That term came later to be applied not to the step exhibited by the Clare dancers but, in a derogatory manner, to the 'universal step' still used indiscriminately for reels, jigs and polkas by some dancers here.)

As people travelled to Ireland to learn and share music, they shared the emergence of the sets as well. There is a well-remembered week in Ennis at Cois na hAbna around 1984, when the local dancers were kind enough to take these New Yorkers aside for several evenings to teach them how to dance sets in the Clare style.

In fact, 1984 could be said to mark the beginning of the spread of interest in the set-dancing revival to New York. Some people saw the sets being danced at the Fleadh Cheoil in Listowel and others went to the classes being given at the Willie Clancy Week. Plans began to be made to invite teachers from Ireland to New York.

When Peter and Winnie Rooney returned from Ireland, they organised the Green Isle *céilí*, at which occasional sets were mixed in with the *céilí* dances. And at the Bedford Hills Céilí, which had started in 1985, the musicians also began to play music for sets intermixed with the *céilí* dances. Peter began to give small workshops in set dancing in 1986, and he invited Jack Slattery to give a series of workshops. Jack's influence could be seen here in New York even a decade later, when the 'Dublin version' of the Cashel Set hornpipe figure was still danced.

At the Willie Clancy Week in 1985, a group also approached Joe Donovan to come to the States to teach sets. He made a six-week tour all the way from Cork, sponsored by the Irish Arts Centre in New York, the Greater Washington Céilí Club, the Philadelphia Céilí Club and the Comhaltas Ceoltóirí Éireann organisation in Boston.

This tour was the first of five teaching tours Joe made, and in 1987 he taught at the first of the Greater Washington Céilí Club's dance weekends at Cape May. Set-dancing opportunities were still limited in the New York area, however. In addition to the occasional sets danced at Green Isle or Bedford Hills, the summer dancing in Central Park included sets, like the North Kerry, that were also danced at the Milltown Lounge in the Bronx. The Milltown was well known for sessions that attracted talented musicians, and the fact that some of the musicians were related to some of the dancers predisposed them to prolong the occasional run of reels or polkas long enough for figures of sets to be danced.

Donncha Ó Múinneacháin was also invited to teach, at the Comhaltas Ceoltóirí Éireann weekend in 1987, and returned to teach many other workshops, especially in the Boston area. And 1987 also saw Connie Ryan's first trip to New York to teach. After that successful trip, he returned to teach the second and subsequent Cape May weekends, which the Greater Washington Céilí Club renamed the Connie Ryan Memorial

Set Dance Weekend after his passing in 1997. In 1991 he brought the Slievenamon dancers with him to tour New York, Washington, Philadelphia, Boston and Springfield. Set-dancing *céilís* started up at places like the Cork Lounge; their playing style and collections of tunes developed to the point where, today, they often suit the set dancing more than the *céilí* dancing. His enthusiasm and energy was returned by that of the growing community of dancers, and his passing was mourned by the dancers here, several of whom travelled to his funeral in Clonoulty – and hundreds of whom turned out for a memorial service held in New York. The circle of dancers widened even further over succeeding years as the popularity of set dancing exploded in the States, as it did in Ireland, so that now, in the late 1990s, the New York area has at least six teachers giving weekly classes, a dozen *céilís* each month and two or three weekend set-dancing festivals each year.

The following article outlining set-dance development in Nova Scotia was provided by Elizabeth MacDonald, an excellent dancer and teacher who has been central to the development of Irish set dancing in the Maritime Provinces of Canada.

Irish Set Dancing in Nova Scotia

The patterns of immigration to Atlantic Canada over the past several hundred years resulted in the region being populated to a large degree by Highland Scots and Irish, who joined the already settled Acadian French in developing a unique musical culture. For people growing up in this part of the country, traditional music, song and dance are part of the fabric of many households, particularly in the more rural areas. The international revival of interest in Celtic music and dance during the 1980s simply brought a broader-based credibility and cachet to an existing traditional culture in Atlantic Canada. Part of this heritage is a style of quadrille-based formation dancing referred to as 'set squares' or simply 'squares'. Found throughout the four Atlantic provinces of Newfoundland, Nova Scotia, Prince Edward Island and New Brunswick, these dances contain elements similar to Irish sets as well as to quadrilles found throughout other parts of rural Canada and the United States.

The origins of the dance form are not certain. It is possible that it travelled with immigrants who arrived in the mid- to late 1800s. An equally plausible explanation, especially since much of the settlement occurred before this time, is that the popular quadrille may have made its way to Atlantic Canada from the eastern seaboard of the United States – these two regions have close trading links. (Earlier this century, for example, Nova Scotian folklorist Helen Creighton found quadrille dances with names like 'The American' and others that are widely understood to have originated in the United States.) Regardless of the combination of influences that created these dances, over time communities developed their own sets, incorporating local footwork, styling and music.

These formation dances, often called lancers and quadrilles, continue to be danced in rural communities throughout the four provinces. Like the Irish sets before the set-dancing revival, however, the squares are slowly being lost with the passing of the generations. Nonetheless, given the already strong traditional music scene in Nova Scotia, Irish set dancing fits naturally into this milieu.

Set and *céilí* dancing were introduced to Nova Scotia in the early 1990s, initially through the efforts of An Cumann: The Irish Association of Nova Scotia. Since 1992, Elizabeth MacDonald has taught set dancing in Halifax, and today her classes attract close to fifty students, from beginner through to advanced. A demonstration team, Scaip na Cleiti (Irish for 'Toss the Feathers', a tribute to Pat Murphy), performs both traditional Irish set dances and choreographed works at special events throughout the province. Over the years, the Halifax set dancers have hosted a number of workshop leaders, including Pat Murphy, Martin Bolger, Aidan Vaughan, Patrick O'Dea, Eileen O'Doherty and Mick Mulkerrin. Elizabeth is currently collecting set-square dances from Nova Scotia, Prince Edward Island and New Brunswick.

NOTES

1 Breandán Breathnach. *Dancing in Ireland*. Dal gCais Publications, Milltown Malbay, County Clare, 1983
2 Seán Donnelly. *Ceol na hÉireann*. Na Píobairí Uilleann, Dublin, 1993
3 Francis Roche. *Collection of Irish Airs. Marches and Dance Tunes*. Dublin, 1927
4 *World History of the Dance*. W. W. Norton & Co Inc. 1937

INDEX OF DANCES

ARMAGH LANCERS SET

This lovely old set, similar to the Second (Lancer) Set of Quadrilles, was given to me by Aleta Hancock from Los Angeles, who learned it from Patrick O'Dea during his workshop there in April 1999.

FIGURE 1: JIG (136 BARS)

(a) Top lady and opposite gent advance and swing in the centre reversing to place during the last two bars.   (8 bars)

(b) Top couples square. They cross over, passing right shoulder to right with the opposite lady or gent, then pass their partner right shoulder to right as they dance through the opposite position. From there, they cross back, again passing right shoulder to right with the opposite lady or gent, and pass their own partners right shoulder to right as they dance through their own positions to face the person in their own corner.   (8 bars)

(c) All swing the lady or gent in their own corner (gent's left, lady's right).   (8 bars)

(d) All swing their own partners in place.   (8 bars)

(e) Top lady and opposite gent advance and swing in the centre, reversing to place during the last two bars.   (8 bars)

(f) Top couples dance the square again.   (8 bars)

(g) All swing the lady or gent in their own corner (gent's left, lady's right).   (8 bars)

(h) All swing their own partners in place.   (8 bars)

(i) Repeat (a) to (h) with side couples leading. First side couple are on the left of first top couple.   (64 bars)

FIGURE 2: JIG OR SINGLE REEL (136 BARS)

(a) First top couple advance to the centre holding right hand in right, and as they retire the lady turns anticlockwise under the gent's arm (4 bars), then they swing in place (4 bars).   (8 bars)

(b) Top couples square. They cross over, passing right shoulder to right with the opposite lady or gent, then pass their partner right shoulder to right as they dance through the opposite position. From there, they cross back, again passing right shoulder to right with the opposite lady or gent, and pass their own partners right shoulder to right as they dance back to their own places and finish facing into the set. During the last two bars, side couples move apart from their partners to line up in top positions, four facing four. Side ladies dance to join the top couple on their right and side gents dance to join the top couple on their left. (8 bars)

(c) All advance and retire twice in the lines of four. (8 bars)

(d) All swing their own partners in place. (8 bars)

(e) Second top couple advance to the centre holding right hand in right, and as they retire the lady turns anticlockwise under the gent's arm (4 bars), then they swing in place (4 bars). (8 bars)

(f) Top couples square. They cross over, passing right shoulder to right with the opposite lady or gent, then pass their partner right shoulder to right as they dance through the opposite position. From there, they cross back, again passing right shoulder to right with the opposite lady or gent, and pass their own partners right shoulder to right as they dance back to their own places and finish facing into the set. During the last two bars, side couples move apart from their partners to line up in top positions, four facing four. Side ladies dance to join the top couple on their right and side gents dance to join the top couple on their left. (8 bars)

(g) All advance and retire twice in the lines of four. (8 bars)

(h) All swing their own partners in place. (8 bars)

(i) Repeat (a) to (h) with side couples leading. First side couple are on the left of first top couple. The line-up is now in side positions, with the top dancers moving apart to line up with the sides. (64 bars)

FIGURE 3: JIG (136 BARS)

(a) Forming a circle of eight, all four couples swing clockwise (4 bars), then anticlockwise (4 bars) (8 bars)

(b) Top couples advance to the centre (2 bars), turn slightly clockwise to face the side couple on their right (2 bars), reverse into opposite positions (2 bars) and turn clockwise to face the other side couple, who are now on their right (2 bars). (8 bars)

(c) Top couples join right hands with the side couple facing them, dance around (4 bars), then join left hands and dance back (4 bars). (8 bars)

(d) Top couples now swing in four with the side couple with whom they joined hands. Top couples finish in opposite position to their own, while side couples finish in their own positions. (8 bars)

(e) Forming a circle of eight, all four couples swing clockwise (4 bars), then anticlockwise (4 bars). (8 bars)

(f) Top couples repeat (b) to (d), joining hands and swinging with the other side couple. They now finish back in their own places. (24 bars)

(g) Repeat (a) to (f) with side couples leading.   (64 bars)

FIGURE 4: JIG (136 BARS)

(a) The four ladies advance and retire twice.   (8 bars)
(b) The four gents advance and retire twice.   (8 bars)
(c) The four ladies join hands in the centre and dance around
    clockwise (4 bars), then join left hands and dance back to place
    (4 bars). While they are dancing this, the four gents dance
    anticlockwise around outside, turning clockwise four times as
    they do so.   (8 bars)
(d) All ladies move on to swing the gent on their right, and they stay
    in that position after the swing.   (8 bars)
(e) Repeat (a) to (d) three times, ladies dancing in each position and
    moving on to the next position on the right each time until they
    are back swinging their own partners again.   (96 bars)

FIGURE 5: JIG OR HORNPIPE (168 BARS)

(a) Taking their partners right hand in right, all dance the grand chain
    all round, gents anticlockwise and ladies clockwise (12 bars).
    When they meet their partners, gents place their right arm around
    the lady's waist and line up facing first top position (4 bars).
    Couple on the left (first side couple this time) are second in line,
    couple on the right (second side couple) are third and second top
    couple are fourth.   (16 bars)
(b) With each lady passing in front of her partner and first top lady
    leading, ladies dance anticlockwise around to the back of the line
    and gents dance clockwise around to the back to meet them, first
    top gent leading. All then lead up the centre with their own
    partners and move apart to line up with the four ladies facing the
    four gents.   (8 bars)
(c) The lines advance and retire twice.   (8 bars)
(d) All advance (2 bars) and swing their partners back to place
    (6 bars).   (8 bars)
(e) Repeat (a) to (d) with second top couple leading. Second side
    couple are second in line this time.   (40 bars)
(f) Repeat (a) to (d) with first side couple leading. Second top couple
    are second in line this time.   (40 bars)
(g) Repeat (a) to (d) with second side couple leading. First top couple
    are second in line this time.   (40 bars)

AUSTRALIAN HALF SET

This set, which is said to have Irish origins, was taught to Jean Ver Hoeven and the Philadelphia Set Dancers by Bill and Margaret Winnett during a visit to the United States. Jean kindly supplied me with their notes from the workshop.

FIGURE 1: JIG OR POLKA (48 BARS)

(a) Taking right hands, each couple cross anticlockwise to opposite positions, with the lady dancing in front. As the lady reverses into the opposite position, she turns clockwise under the gent's arm.　(4 bars)

(b) Repeat (a), crossing back to home.　(4 bars)

(c) Both couples swing in *céilí* hold, holding their partner's upper right arm instead of holding left hands.　(8 bars)

(d) Ladies chain with right hands in the centre, turn around opposite gent with left hand, then dance into a line of four with the other couple, ladies holding hands in the centre, and dance on the spot.　(8 bars)

(e) Ladies dance home and swing their partners.　(8 bars)

(f) Both couples house around in *céilí* hold.　(8 bars)

FIGURE 2: JIG OR POLKA (64 BARS)

(a) Taking right hands, each couple advance and retire once, then cross anticlockwise to opposite positions, with the lady dancing in front. As the lady reverses into the opposite position, she turns clockwise under the gent's arm.　(8 bars)

(b) Repeat (a), crossing back to home.　(8 bars)

(c) Both couples swing in *céilí* hold, holding their partner's upper right arm instead of holding left hands.　(8 bars)

(d) Repeat (a) to (c).　(24 bars)

(e) Both couples house around in *céilí* hold.　(8 bars)

FIGURE 3: JIG OR POLKA (64 BARS)

(a) First top gent and second top lady swing in the centre while their partners sidestep in place, dancing 'sevens' and 'threes'.　(8 bars)

(b) Each of the dancers in the centre takes their own partner's right hand in their right hand and cross to opposite positions, where each lady turns clockwise under her partner's right arm. They repeat the movement back to home.　(8 bars)

(c) Both couples swing in *céilí* hold, holding their partner's upper right arm instead of holding left hands. (8 bars)

(d) Repeat (a) to (c) with the first top lady and opposite gent leading. (24 bars)

(e) Both couples house around in *céilí* hold. (8 bars)

FIGURE 4: JIG OR POLKA (128 BARS)

(a) Ladies chain with right hands in the centre, turn around opposite gent with left hand, then dance into a line of four with the other couple, ladies holding hands in the centre, and dance on the spot. (8 bars)

(b) Ladies dance home and swing their partners. (8 bars)

(c) First top couple house across and leave the lady with the second couple. While they are crossing, the second couple sidestep to the right, dancing 'sevens', dance two 'threes' on the spot, then dance 'sevens' back to place and dance 'threes' again. (8 bars)

(d) The two ladies face the top gent and take his hands, then all dance to the centre and back twice, the ladies turning out during the last two bars and giving their hands to the second man. All dance to the centre and back again, then advance to the centre. Ladies turn out and form a basket, all hands low around the waist. (16 bars)

(e) All four swing in the basket. (8 bars)

(f) Repeat (a) to (e) with second couple leading. (48 bars)

(g) All dance (a) and (b) again. (16 bars)

(h) Both couples house around in *céilí* hold. (8 bars)

FIGURE 5: JIG OR POLKA (96 BARS)

(a) In waltz hold, both couples dance around the house. (8 bars)

(b) Both couples gallop (hop 1 2 3 4 5 6 7) to the centre and back, then house across to opposite positions. (8 bars)

(c) Repeat (b), dancing back to home. (8 bars)

(d) Ladies chain with right hands in the centre, turn around opposite gent with left hand, then dance into a line of four with the other couple, ladies holding hands in the centre, and dance on the spot. (8 bars)

(e) Ladies dance home and swing their partners. (8 bars)

(f) Both couples house around in *céilí* hold. (8 bars)

(g) Repeat (b) to (f). (40 bars)

FIGURE 6: JIG OR POLKA

(a) All half-sets get together in one big circle, then advance and retire twice. (8 bars)

(b) All swing their own partners. (8 bars)

(c) All couples house anticlockwise around the circle for eight bars. (8 bars)

(d) All circle, advance and retire, then advance again and ladies move on to the next gent on their right. (8 bars)

(e) All swing their new partners. (8 bars)

(f) All house with their new partners. (8 bars)

(g) Repeat (d) to (f) until all house with their own partners again.

BALLINGEARY JIG SET

This traditional set from west Cork is danced to slides. I first learned it at a class in the Pipers' Club in Dublin. It has previously been published by Eileen O'Doherty in her set-dancing collection The Walking Polka.

FIGURE 1: SLIDE (120 BARS)

(a) Body: All couples take waltz hold, slide to the centre (1 2, 1 2 3), slide back (1 2, 1 2 3) and turn clockwise twice as they move to the position on their right. They then repeat the movements three times as they dance around the set to home. (32 bars)

(b) Top couples house inside. (8 bars)

(c) Top couples square forward to the position on their right and reverse to the positions opposite their own (4 bars). They repeat the movements back to their own places. (8 bars)

(d) Top couples swing in place. (8 bars)

(e) All couples dance the body movements to the position opposite their own. (16 bars)

(f) From opposite positions, side couples dance (b) to (d). (24 bars)

(g) All couples dance the body movements again, dancing back to their own places. (16 bars)

FIGURE 2: SLIDE (136 BARS)

(a) Body: All couples take waltz hold, slide to the centre (1 2, 1 2 3), slide back (1 2, 1 2 3) and turn clockwise twice as they move to the position on their right. They then repeat the movements three times as they dance around the set to home. (32 bars)

(b) Top couples house inside. (8 bars)

(c) Top couples square forward to the position on their right and reverse to the positions opposite their own (4 bars). They repeat the movements back to their own places. (8 bars)

(d) Top gents dance straight across and swing in place with opposite ladies. (8 bars)

(e) Top gents dance straight across and swing in place with their own partners. (8 bars)

(f) All couples dance the body movements to the position opposite their own. (16 bars)

(g) From opposite positions, side couples dance (b) to (e). (32 bars)

(h) All couples dance the body movements again, dancing back to their own places. (16 bars)

FIGURE 3: SLIDE (152 BARS)

(a) Body: All couples take waltz hold, slide to the centre (1 2, 1 2 3), slide back (1 2, 1 2 3) and turn clockwise twice as they move to the position on their right. They then repeat the movements three times as they dance around the set to home. (32 bars)

(b) Top couples house inside. (8 bars)

(c) Top couples square forward to the position on their right and reverse to the positions opposite their own (4 bars). They repeat the movements back to their own places. (8 bars)

(d) The four ladies join right hands in the centre and dance around, then join left hands and dance back to place. (8 bars)

(e) The four gents join right hands in the centre and dance around, then join left hands and dance back to place. (8 bars)

(f) All couples swing in place. (8 bars)

(g) All couples dance the body movements to the position opposite their own. (16 bars)

(h) From opposite positions, side couples dance (b) and (c), then all dance (d) to (f). (40 bars)

(i) All couples dance the body movements again, dancing back to their own places. (16 bars)

FIGURE 4: SLIDE (168 BARS)

(a) Body: All couples take waltz hold, slide to the centre (1 2, 1 2 3), slide back (1 2, 1 2 3) and turn clockwise twice as they move to the position on their right. They then repeat the movements three times as they dance around the set to home. (32 bars)

(b) Top couples house inside. (8 bars)

(c) Top couples square forward to the position on their right and reverse to the positions opposite their own (4 bars). They repeat the movements back to their own places. (8 bars)

(d) Top gents swing with each lady in turn, starting with the lady on their left and moving left each time until back swinging their own partners. (32 bars)

(e) All couples dance the body movements to the position opposite their own. (16 bars)

(f) From opposite positions, side couples dance (b) to (d). (48 bars)

(g) All couples dance the body movements again, dancing back to their own places. (16 bars)

FIGURE 5: SLIDE (136 BARS)

(a) Body: All couples take waltz hold, slide to the centre (1 2, 1 2 3), slide back (1 2, 1 2 3) and turn clockwise twice as they move to the position on their right. They then repeat the movements three times as they dance around the set to home. (32 bars)

(b) Top couples house inside. (8 bars)

(c) Top couples square forward to the position on their right and reverse to the positions opposite their own (4 bars). They repeat the movements back to their own places. (8 bars)

(d) Facing their partners and taking right hand in right, all dance a half-turn into their partner's position so that they are facing back towards their own. Then all chain halfway around the set, gents clockwise and ladies anticlockwise. (8 bars)

(e) All couples swing in opposite positions. (8 bars)

(f) Starting in opposite positions, all couples dance the body movements back to their own places. (16 bars)

(g) Side couples dance (b) and (c). (16 bars)

(h) Facing their partners and taking right hand in right, all dance a half-turn into their partner's position so that they are facing back towards their own. Then all chain halfway around the set, gents clockwise and ladies anticlockwise. (8 bars)

(i) All couples swing in opposite positions. (8 bars)

(j) All couples dance the body movements again, dancing back to their own places. (16 bars)

BALLYCROY SET

This lovely traditional set comes from Ballycroy, Westport, County Mayo. I learned it from Martin Murray on 6 August 1999 during a fine night's dancing in Michael and Mary Corcoran's house in Renmore, County Galway. Martin, who is Mary's father, travelled from Logduff, Ballycroy, to teach us the set.

FIGURE 1: JIG (224 BARS)

(a) Taking their partner's nearest hand, all couples lead around clockwise, gents leading the ladies (12 bars), and dance out facing their partners (4 bars). (16 bars)

(b) All couples swing in waltz hold. (8 bars)

(c) Top ladies chain. They take right hands in the centre and turn clockwise under the opposite gent's left arm, dancing anticlockwise around him as he moves forward slightly and reverses into place again without turning. They then chain back, taking right hands again, and turn under their own partner's arm in the same way. (8 bars)

(d) Top couples swing in place. (8 bars)

(e) Side couples dance (c) and (d). (16 bars)

(f) Top gents cross over, passing left shoulder to left (2 bars), dance facing the opposite lady (2 bars) and swing with her (4 bars). (8 bars)

(g) Top couples dance the polka 'sevens' to the centre and back, then house across to the opposite position, turning twice. (8 bars)

(h) Top couples repeat (g), crossing back to the ladies' home positions. (8 bars)

(i) Top gents cross home (2 bars), dance facing their own partners (2 bars) and swing with them (4 bars). (8 bars)

(j) Top couples dance the polka 'sevens' to the centre and back, then house across to the opposite position, turning twice. (8 bars)

(k) Top couples repeat (j), crossing back home. (8 bars)

(l) Side couples dance (f) to (k). (48 bars)

(m) Taking their partner's nearest hand, all couples lead around anticlockwise, ladies leading the gents (12 bars), and dance out facing their partners (4 bars). (16 bars)

(n) All couples swing in waltz hold. (8 bars)

(o) Top ladies chain. They take right hands in the centre and turn clockwise under the opposite gent's left arm, dancing anticlockwise around him as he moves forward slightly and reverses into place again without turning. They then chain back, taking right hands again in the centre, turn under their own partner's arm in the same way and move to the centre, forming a circle of four. (8 bars)

(p) Top couples swing in the basket (four together) in the centre (6 bars) and reverse back to place (2 bars). (8 bars)

(q) Side couples dance (o) and (p). (16 bars)

(r) Facing their own partners, all dance out (4 bars) and swing (4 bars). (8 bars)

FIGURE 2: POLKA (184 BARS)

(a) Taking waltz hold, top couples dance the long polka, or 'sevens'. Starting by stepping onto their inside (gent's left, lady's right) foot, they dance double sevens across the set, going around the other couple and then, changing to lead on their other foot (gent's right, lady's left), they dance another double sevens back to their place. Each time, they keep almost all of their weight on the leading foot. (8 bars)

(b) Top couples house around each other. (8 bars)

(c) Top ladies chain, as in Figure 1, and form a circle of four in the centre. (8 bars)

(d) Top couples swing in the basket (four together) in the centre (6 bars) and reverse back to place (2 bars). (8 bars)

(e) Side couples dance (a) to (d). (32 bars)

(f) All gents face the lady on their left in the corner and they take two hands, dancing all the time (2 bars). They then turn clockwise together one and a half times so that the lady finishes in the lady's position to the right of her own (6 bars). (8 bars)

(g) Top gents and new partners dance (a) to (d). (32 bars)

(h) Side gents and new partners dance (a) to (d). (32 bars)

(i) Facing their new partners, all dance on the spot, taking both hands crossed (2 bars), then turn anticlockwise one and a half times, the ladies finishing back in their original places (6 bars). (8 bars)

(j) All dance to their partners (2 bars) and swing (6 bars). (8 bars)

(k) Top ladies chain again while side couples take right arm in right and turn clockwise twice in place. (8 bars)

(l) Side ladies chain again, while top couples take right arm in right and turn clockwise twice in place. (8 bars)

(m) All dance out to their partners (2 bars) and swing (6 bars). (8 bars)

FIGURE 3: REEL (184 BARS)

(a) Taking hands in a circle, all face to their left and dance clockwise (4 bars), then turn to face to their right and dance anticlockwise back to place (4 bars). (8 bars)

(b) Taking hands in a circle, all face to their right and dance anticlockwise (4 bars), then turn to face to their left and dance clockwise back to place (4 bars). (8 bars)

(c) Changing to waltz hold with their partners, all couples dance reel sevens to the centre and back, then house anticlockwise to opposite positions, turning clockwise twice as they cross. (8 bars)

(d) All couples dance reel sevens to the centre and back, then house anticlockwise to their home positions, again turning clockwise twice. (8 bars)

(e) The four ladies dance across to the next lady's position on their right. Facing the gent, they take his right hand in right as they pass inside him, then they dance one full turn clockwise around each other. (8 bars)

(f) All repeat (c) to (e) three times as the ladies move around the set, dancing with each gent in turn, then arrive back to their own partners. (72 bars)

(g) All swing their own partners. (8 bars)

(h) All repeat (a) and (b). (16 bars)

(i) All chain around the set, gents anticlockwise and ladies clockwise. Taking their partner's right hand in right, holding the hands up palm to palm, all dance one full clockwise turn (4 bars), then take left hands with the next person and dance one full turn anticlockwise (4 bars) and repeat these turns with each person as they chain all round the set. (32 bars)

(j) All swing their partners to finish. (8 bars)

BALLYROAN HALF SET

(COUNTY LAOIS)

This traditional half-set has been danced in competition by the Ballyroan Set Dancers for over twenty years. The dancers are Eileen and Brendan Reilly and Helen and Paddy Cahill. In putting the set together, they had much help and encouragement from Maura Shanahan, Richie Lyons and Noreen Fogarty.

FIGURE 1: POLKA (120 BARS)

(a) In waltz hold, both couples slide to the centre and back (4 bars), then turn clockwise once to the next position on their right (2 bars) and dance on the spot there, still in waltz hold (2 bars). These movements are repeated three times as they dance around the set to home (24 bars). (32 bars)

(b) Both couples swing in waltz hold, dancing out the last bar to face into the set. (8 bars)

(c) Holding their hands fairly high, the ladies chain with right arms in the centre, turn with left arm around opposite gent and dance back, right shoulder to right, to take their own partner's right hand and face forward into the set. (8 bars)

(d) Holding right hands, both couples advance and retire once (4 bars), then cross on the right to opposite positions with each lady in front of the gent, turning clockwise twice under his right arm. (8 bars)

(e) Repeat (d), crossing back to home. (8 bars)

(f) The gents dance forward, passing each other right shoulder to right in the centre, and reverse back, passing left shoulder to left (6 bars), then cross, again passing right shoulder to right, and turn in anticlockwise to place their right arm over opposite lady's shoulder, take both hands and face forward towards the other couple (2 bars). (8 bars)

(g) Both couples dance forward anticlockwise into a line of four in the position on their right and dance on the spot there (4 bars), then continue anticlockwise to face in from the gent's own original position, gents bringing their right arm forward over the lady's head (4 bars). (8 bars)

(h) The gents dance forward, passing each other right shoulder to right in the centre, and reverse back, passing left shoulder to left

(6 bars), then cross, again passing right shoulder to right, and turn in anticlockwise to place their right arm over their own partner's shoulder in the opposite position, take both hands and face forward towards the other couple (2 bars). (8 bars)

(i) Both couples dance forward anticlockwise into a line of four in the position on their right and dance on the spot there (4 bars), then continue anticlockwise to face in from their own original positions (4 bars). (8 bars)

(j) Both couples advance and retire twice holding right hands. (8 bars)

(k) Both couples swing. (8 bars)

FIGURE 2: JIG (128 BARS)

(a) Taking hands in a circle, the four dancers advance (1 2 3, 1 2 3) and retire (step, batter, step, batter, step, batter, step, batter). Gents start the retire by stepping back on the left foot and battering on the right, while ladies start by stepping back on the right foot and battering on the left (4 bars). While the gents turn slightly clockwise, ladies now reverse back outside their partners into a line of four, with each couple facing anticlockwise. All dance the same steps as in the circle when forming this line (4 bars), and in the line each gent has his arm around the lady's waist while she rests her left hand on his shoulder. (8 bars)

(b) All advance to the next position (1 2 3, 1 2 3) and dance on the spot, retire (step, batter, step, batter, step, batter, step, batter), then repeat, moving on to face in from the opposite position. (8 bars)

(c) Starting in opposite positions and finishing at home, all repeat (a) and (b). (16 bars)

(d) Taking nearest (inside) hands, both couples advance (1 2 3, 1 2 3) and retire (battering), then cross to opposite side, with first couple making an arch and second couple passing under the arch as they cross. At the opposite side, all turn in to their partners and take their other hand to face back. Each lady is now in opposite gent's position, while each gent is in opposite lady's position. (8 bars)

(e) Repeat (d), with second couple making the arch this time and first couple passing under it as they cross back. (8 bars)

(f) Still holding inside hands, both couples advance and retire once, then gents cross, passing right shoulder to right, and turn in to face the opposite lady. (8 bars)

(g) All swing new partner (7 bars) and dance the last bar into a straight line, with each couple facing anticlockwise across the set. (8 bars)

(h) All advance to the next position (1 2 3, 1 2 3) and dance on the spot, retire (step, batter, step, batter, step, batter, step, batter), then repeat, moving on to face in from the opposite position.   (8 bars)

(i) Repeat (f) to (h), all finishing back in place with their own partners.   (24 bars)

(j) Both couples advance and retire, then advance again and form a circle in the centre, with the ladies resting their hands on the gents' shoulders.   (8 bars)

(k) All swing in four in the centre, then break away to swing their own partners in place. They usually finish by dancing out the last bar.   (16 bars)

FIGURE 3: HORNPIPE (112 BARS)

(a) Taking waltz hold and standing to the side of their partners, all dance one full forward turn clockwise in place (hop, tap 1, tap 2, tap 3, three times, then hop 1 2 3).   (4 bars)

(b) Gents now move on to their right while ladies move on to their left to face the next person in side positions (hop, tap 1, tap 2, tap 3 twice), then dance facing the next person (1 2 3 and clap three times).   (4 bars)

(c) All repeat the movements in (a) and (b), turning with this partner and moving on again to face their own partners in the opposite position.   (8 bars)

(d) All repeat (a) to (c), dancing around the set to home.   (16 bars)

(e) All repeat (a) with their own partners in place, then gents cross, passing left shoulder to left to face opposite lady (hop, tap 1, tap 2, tap 3 twice) and dance facing her (1 2 3 and clap three times).   (8 bars)

(f) All repeat (a) with new partners, then double across in waltz hold to the gent's original position and dance the last two bars facing each other there. Ladies are now in the opposite lady's position.   (8 bars)

(g) All repeat (a) with their new partners in place, then gents cross, passing left shoulder to left to face their own partners in the opposite positions (hop, tap 1, tap 2, tap 3 twice) and dance facing them (1 2 3 and clap three times).   (8 bars)

(h) All repeat (a) with their own partners, then double across in waltz hold to their own original position and dance the last two bars facing each other there.   (8 bars)

(i) Repeat (e) to (h) with the ladies crossing over this time instead of the gents. As they cross each time, they pass right shoulder to right.   (32 bars)

(j) All repeat (a) and dance out the last four bars on the spot alone, facing forward into the set. (8 bars)

FIGURE 4: POLKA (136 BARS)

(a) Taking waltz hold, both couples slide to the centre and back, then turn clockwise twice as they cross anticlockwise to opposite positions. (8 bars)

(b) Repeat (a), dancing back home. (8 bars)

(c) Facing forward, all pass through to opposite positions, with each lady passing between opposite couple, and turn in towards their partners to face back (4 bars). All dance back to form a line of four in the centre, gents turning anticlockwise to stand beside the opposite lady in the line (outside her) and face the same way as her (towards her position). He now takes her left hand in his left and his own partner's right hand in his right over the new partner's shoulder. (8 bars)

(d) In this line, all dance a half-turn until each gent and opposite lady are facing towards the gent's side of the set (4 bars), then, releasing their own partner's hand, each gent and new partner, side by side, turn anticlockwise and reverse into the gent's position, the gent bringing his hand forward over the lady's head during the last bar (4 bars). (8 bars)

(e) All repeat (c) and (d), ladies starting in opposite positions and all finishing back in their own positions. (16 bars)

(f) Holding right hand in right, all advance and retire once, then advance again, and top gent takes opposite lady's left hand and turns her clockwise in beside him, bringing his hand forward over her head as all retire. (8 bars)

(g) As the top gent and both ladies face the second gent, all advance and retire again, then advance, and the second gent takes the ladies' free hands and pulls them towards him, bringing his hands back low, then forward over their heads as they turn and all retire again. (8 bars)

(h) All advance and retire again, then advance, and top gent takes the ladies' free hands and pulls them towards him, bringing his hands over their heads as the ladies turn to face into the set. (8 bars)

(i) All swing in four in the centre, ladies resting their hands on the gents' shoulders. (8 bars)

(j) All break from the swing to swing their own partners in place. (8 bars)

(k) All advance and retire again, then advance and, with the ladies crossing their hands, right over left, all take hands in a circle. (8 bars)

(l) All dance on the spot in the circle. (8 bars)

(m) Still holding the gents' hands, the ladies raise their hands and turn clockwise to face out of the circle and all dance on the spot again.

(8 bars)

(n) Ladies turn anticlockwise to face in with their hands crossed and all dance on the spot again. (8 bars)

(o) All swing their own partners to finish. (8 bars)

BORLIN JENNY REEL SET

This set comes from the Borlin Valley area of County Cork. It was revived by Olive Lynch of Bantry and a slightly different version was taught by dancing teacher Timmy MacCarthy at the Galway International Set Dancing Festival in 1998. Gentle reel steps are danced, except for the square, where all dance a lively 'skip' reel step.

FIGURE 1: REEL (96 BARS)
(a) All couples lead around holding right hands.   (8 bars)
(b) All couples advance and retire twice holding right hand in right. (8 bars)
(c) Top couples dance the star with the side couple on their right, joining right hands (4 bars) and left hands (4 bars).   (8 bars)
(d) All couples dance the square in waltz hold: the gents dance forward as the ladies reverse to the position on the right, dance two bars on the spot turning slightly, then gents reverse as the ladies dance forward to the next position, dance two bars there and repeat all the movements as they continue dancing around the set to home. (Another way of dancing this square is for the ladies to dance forward beside the gents during the first and third part of the square; they also dance forward during the second and fourth parts.)   (16 bars)
(e) All couples house around.   (8 bars)
(f) Repeat (b) to (e), all couples dancing the star (c) with the couple on the other side this time.   (40 bars)

FIGURE 2: REEL (96 BARS)
(a) All couples lead around holding right hands.   (8 bars)
(b) All couples advance and retire once, right hand in right. As they retire, gents bring their right arm back over the lady's head to rest it on her shoulder and lead anticlockwise to the opposite position, where ladies turn clockwise to face into the set.   (8 bars)
(c) All couples repeat (b), dancing back to home.   (8 bars)
(d) All couples square, as in Figure 1 (d).   (16 bars)
(e) All couples house around.   (8 bars)
(f) Repeat (b) to (e).   (40 bars)

FIGURE 3: REEL (96 BARS)

(a) All couples lead around holding right hands.   (8 bars)

(b) All couples advance and retire once, right hand in right (4 bars) then gents swing with the lady on their left (4 bars).   (8 bars)

(c) All advance and retire once with their new partner (4 bars), then dance back to their own partners and swing.   (8 bars)

(d) All couples square, as in Figure 1 (d).   (16 bars)

(e) All couples house around.   (8 bars)

(f) Repeat (b) to (e).   (40 bars)

FIGURE 4: REEL (80 BARS)

(a) All couples lead around holding crossed hands.   (8 bars)

(b) All sidestep past their own partner, dance for two bars on the spot, sidestep back to place and dance for two bars again. Whichever partner is dancing to the right passes behind the other partner.   (8 bars)

(c) All couples square, as in Figure 1 (d).   (16 bars)

(d) All couples house around.   (8 bars)

(e) Repeat (b) to (d).   (32 bars)

FIGURE 5: REEL (112 BARS)

(a) All couples lead around holding crossed hands.   (8 bars)

(b) Holding their partner's right hand, all turn clockwise to their partner's position, then chain all round, gents dancing clockwise and ladies anticlockwise.   (16 bars)

(c) All couples swing in home positions.   (8 bars)

(d) All couples square, as in Figure 1 (d).   (16 bars)

(e) All couples house around.   (8 bars)

(f) Repeat (b) to (e).   (48 bars)

FIGURE 6: REEL (112 BARS)

(a) All couples lead around holding crossed hands.   (8 bars)

(b) The four ladies join right hands in the centre, dance around halfway, join left hands and dance back to place.   (8 bars)

(c) The four gents join right hands in the centre, dance around halfway, join left hands and dance back to place.   (8 bars)

(d) Keeping their left hands in the centre, each gent places his right arm around the lady, she places her left hand on his shoulder and all lead around.   (8 bars)

(e) All couples square, as in Figure 1 (d).   (16 bars)

(f) All couples house around.   (8 bars)
(g) Repeat (b) to (f).   (48 bars)

BRUCA SET

This set was recorded by Connie Ryan and Betty McCoy during a display of Mayo sets in Newport in 1994. Betty kindly provided me with their recording of the set and Ciarán Condron gave me his notes. The set was danced in the Ballintubber, Partry, Clogher, Tourmakeady and Bruca areas and was given to the Newport Dancers by Nora Burke. The step for the last figure is a single hop to each bar of music, ladies starting on the right foot and gents on the left. The breakdown of bars is approximate, but the full chaining sequence always takes twelve bars.

FIGURE 1: JIG (320 BARS)

(a) Top couples square. They take crossed hands, dance to face the couple on their left and reverse to opposite positions, dance left again and reverse back home. (8 bars)

(b) Top couples swing in *céilí* hold. (8 bars)

(c) Top ladies chain. They take right arms in the centre, turn with left arm around the opposite gent and dance back to place. (8 bars)

(d) Top couples swing in *céilí* hold. (8 bars)

(e) Taking crossed hands again, top couples advance and retire twice. (8 bars)

(f) Top couples square to opposite positions. (4 bars)

(g) Taking crossed hands again, top couples advance and retire twice. (8 bars)

(h) Top couples square back to home positions. (4 bars)

(i) Top couples swing in *céilí* hold. (8 bars)

(j) Side couples dance (a) to (i). (64 bars)

(k) While top gent and opposite lady swing in the centre, their partners cross, passing right shoulder to right, turn clockwise in opposite positions, pass back right shoulder to right and turn into place, with the lady turning clockwise and the gent anticlockwise. (8 bars)

(l) Taking crossed hands again, top couples advance and retire twice. (8 bars)

(m) Top lady and opposite gent swing while their partners cross over and back. (8 bars)

(n) Taking crossed hands again, top couples advance and retire twice. (8 bars)

(o) Top couples swing in *céilí* hold. (8 bars)

(p) Top ladies chain. They take right arms in the centre, turn with left arm around opposite gent and dance back to place. (8 bars)

(q) Top couples swing in *céilí* hold. (8 bars)

(r) Top couples swing in four in the centre. (8 bars)

(s) Top ladies chain. They take right arms in the centre, turn with left arm around opposite gent and dance back to place. (8 bars)

(t) Top couples swing in *céilí* hold. (8 bars)

(u) Top couples swing in four in the centre. (8 bars)

(v) Side couples repeat (k) to (u). (88 bars)

(w) All couples swing in place.

FIGURE 2: POLKA (200 BARS)

(a) Top couples take waltz hold and dance 'sevens' to the centre and back twice. (8 bars)

(b) Top couples house around each other. (8 bars)

(c) Top couples dance sevens to the centre and back twice. (8 bars)

(d) Top couples house around each other again. (8 bars)

(e) Top ladies chain, taking right arms in the centre and left arm with opposite gent as they dance around him, before passing right shoulder to right on the way back home. (8 bars)

(f) Top couples swing in *céilí* hold. (8 bars)

(g) Side couples dance (a) to (f). (48 bars)

(h) Repeat (a) to (g). Top couples and side couples dance again, with all couples dancing (f) the last time. (96 bars)

FIGURE 3: SLIP JIG (88 BARS)

(a) Taking his right arm in her right, the top lady turns once clockwise around her own partner, then moves to the left to turn anticlockwise, left arm in left with the first side gent (4 bars). She then turns clockwise around her own partner again and continues across the set to turn anticlockwise, left arm in left around the opposite top gent (4 bars). Finally she turns clockwise around her own partner again and continues to the right to turn anticlockwise around the second side gent and finish back beside her own partner (4 bars) as all other couples turn into the lead-around position, with each gent holding his partner's right hand behind her back. (12 bars)

(b) All couples lead around. (8 bars)

(c) First side lady repeats (a). She turns clockwise around her own partner and anticlockwise around the second top gent, then clockwise around her own partner and anticlockwise around the second side gent. Finally she turns clockwise around her own partner and anticlockwise around the first top gent as all take the lead-around position again. (12 bars)

(d) All couples lead around. (8 bars)

(e) Second top lady repeats (a). She turns clockwise around her own partner and anticlockwise around the second side gent, then clockwise around her own partner and anticlockwise around the first top gent. Finally she turns clockwise around her own partner and anticlockwise around the second side gent as all take the lead-around position again. (12 bars)

(f) All couples lead around. (8 bars)

(g) Second side lady repeats (a). She turns clockwise around her own partner and anticlockwise around the first top gent, then clockwise around her own partner and anticlockwise around the first side gent. Finally she turns clockwise around her own partner and anticlockwise around the second top gent as all take the lead-around position again. (12 bars)

(h) All couples lead around. (8 bars)

CLOGHAN SET

As described by dancing teacher Tommy Gannon of Ferbane, County Offaly.

FIGURE 1 : REELS (72 BARS)

(a) Top couples pass through with ladies in the centre. Then all dancers turn clockwise and pass back with gents in the centre, then turn clockwise again to face partners and swing in waltz hold. (16 bars)

(b) Top ladies chain with right hands, dance anticlockwise around opposite gent, turning clockwise on his left arm (he does not turn), chain on the way back and dance around partner, turning under his left arm, as he stays facing in also. (8 bars)

(c) Top couples swing again. (8 bars)

(d) Side couples repeat (a) to (d). (32 bars)

FIGURE 2 : REELS (200 BARS)

(a) Top gent and opposite lady dance clockwise around each other to face towards their own positions (2 bars) and swing (6 bars). (8 bars)

(b) Top couples lead around anticlockwise, with each gent's right arm over his partner's shoulder, holding both hands in front. (8 bars)

(c) Top couples take partner's right hand and beat it out. They dance on the spot facing each other and swing. (16 bars)

(d) Top ladies chain as in the first figure. (8 bars)

(e) Top couples swing. (8 bars)

(f) Top couples repeat (a) to (e), second couple dancing (a) (48 bars)

(g) Side couples dance (a) to (f). (96 bars)

FIGURE 3 : REELS (72 BARS)

(a) Top ladies chain. (8 bars)

(b) Top couples swing. (8 bars)

(c) Top gents place their hands on their partner's waist and the ladies place their hands on the gent's shoulders. Both couples ' gallop' – that is, they dance 'sevens' across on the right, 'threes' on the spot, sevens back to place on the same side and threes on the spot again. (8 bars)

(d) Both couples swing in place. (Tommy mentioned that they sometimes danced the swing in four.) (8 bars)

(e) Top couples repeat (a) to (d). (32 bars)

FIGURE 4: REELS (96 BARS)
(a) All circle, advance and retire twice. (8 bars)
(b) All lead around with the gent's right arm over the lady's shoulder, holding both hands. (8 bars)
(c) Swing in place. (8 bars)
(d) Ladies move on to the right and lead around with the next gent. (8 bars)
(e) Repeat (c) and (d) until leading around with own partners again. (48 bars)
(f) All circle, advance and retire to finish. (8 bar)

CLOONAGH LANCERS SET

This set comes from Maugherow in County Sligo. It was taught by Sligo dancing teacher Brenda O'Callaghan at the Keadue Harp Festival in 1997.

FIGURE 1: POLKA (104 BARS)

(a) Top gent and opposite lady dance to the centre, passing left shoulder to left, turn clockwise (4 bars) and swing in waltz hold. (8 bars)

(b) Still holding hands (gent's left in lady's right), the swinging couple give their partners their free hand and lead anticlockwise around the set to their own places. (8 bars)

(c) All turn from their partners to swing the person on the other side, dancing back to their partners during the last bar. (8 bars)

(d) Repeat (a) to (c) with top lady and second top gent dancing (a). (24 bars)

(e) Repeat (a) to (d) with side couples leading. First side couple are on the left-hand side of first top couple. (48 bars)

FIGURE 2: REEL (168 BARS)

(a) Top couples advance and retire twice holding crossed hands. (8 bars)

(b) Top couples house around each other, moving anticlockwise as they turn clockwise, Connemara-style. (8 bars)

(c) Top couples advance and retire twice holding crossed hands. (8 bars)

(d) Top couples house around each other, moving clockwise as they turn anticlockwise, Connemara-style. (8 bars)

(e) Top couples swing in waltz hold. (8 bars)

(f) Side couples dance (a) to (e). (40 bars)

(g) Repeat (a) to (f). (80 bars)

FIGURE 3: REEL (168 BARS)

(a) All face their partners, take right hand in right and chain all round the set (12 bars), then swing in place (4 bars). (16 bars)

(b) First top couple take right hand in right. The lady turns clockwise three times as she moves in front of the gent to his left (6 bars) and they then face each other and back away to line up in side positions (2 bars). During the last two bars, the opposite top couple also line up in side positions, while the side gent on the left and the side lady on the right change places, crossing left shoulder to left, so that the four ladies finish facing the four gents. (8 bars)

(c) All advance and retire twice in the lines. (8 bars)

(d) All dance back to their own places (4 bars) and swing (4 bars). (8 bars)

(e) Repeat (a) to (d) with second top couple leading. (40 bars)

(f) Repeat (a) to (e) with each side couple leading in turn. (80 bars)

FIGURE 4: POLKA (88 BARS)

(a) All advance and retire twice, holding hands in a circle, ladies moving on to the gent on her right during the last two bars. (8 bars)

(b) All dance around the house with their new partners. (8 bars)

(c) Repeat (a) and (b) until ladies are back housing with their own partners again. (48 bars)

(d) Gents lock hands across the centre, right hand over left (2 bars), ladies link arms with their own partners and the gent on their right (2 bars) and all swing in the centre (12 bars). (16 bars)

CUILMORE SET

I am indebted to Ciarán Condron of Dublin for this west Mayo set. Ciarán learned the set from John Joe Geraghty and the Newport Dancers from County Mayo. The jig and slide figures are danced smoothly while the polka and reel are lively.

FIGURE 1: JIG (200 BARS)

(a) Taking crossed hands, top couples lead anticlockwise around the set to home. (8 bars)

(b) Top couples dance on the spot (2 bars) and swing in waltz hold. (8 bars)

(c) Top ladies move to the centre facing their partners, taking crossed hands. Top couples dance clockwise around the set, ladies reversing and gents going forward. (8 bars)

(d) Top couples dance on the spot (2 bars) and swing in waltz hold. (8 bars)

(e) Side couples dance (a) to (d). (32 bars)

(f) Top ladies chain with right hands, turn with left arm around opposite gent and dance back home. (8 bars)

(g) Top gent and opposite lady dance (walk) in to face each other in the centre (2 bars), then dance for two bars and swing (12 bars). (16 bars)

(h) Top couples repeat (c). (8 bars)

(i) Top couples repeat (f) to (h), top lady and second gent leading. (32 bars)

(j) Side couples dance (f) to (i). First side couple are on the left. (64 bars)

FIGURE 3 : SLIDE (136 BARS)

(a) Top couples lead around holding crossed hands. During the last two bars, top gent raises his right arm over the lady's head to rest it on her shoulder. (8 bars)

(b) First top couple cross and the gent takes the opposite lady's left hand as she turns in beside him to cross back to top position. The steps danced when crossing over and back are 1 2 3 4, 1 2, 1 2 3.(8 bars)

(c) The top gent and the two ladies advance to meet the opposite gent (2 bars) and swing in four, moving to the centre (12 bars), and all reverse back to place (2 bars). (16 bars)

(d) Top couples repeat (a) to (c) with second couple leading. (32 bars)

(e) Side couples dance (a) to (e). (64 bars)

FIGURE 3 : POLKA (200 BARS)

(a) Top couples dance 'sevens' across the set, gents passing back to back. They dance fourteen steps on the way over, with gents starting by stepping onto the left foot and ladies onto the right. Changing weight to the other foot, they dance sevens back to place, ladies passing back to back this time. (8 bars)

(b) Top couples house around each other. (8 bars)

(c) Top couples repeat (a) and (b). (16 bars)

(d) Top ladies chain. (8 bars)

(e) Top couples dance at home in waltz hold. (8 bars)

(f) Side couples dance (a) to (e). (48 bars)

(g) Top couples repeat (a) to (d), then swing. (48 bars)

(h) Side couples repeat (a) to (d), then all couples swing. (48 bars)

FIGURE 4: REEL (168 BARS)

(a) Holding hands in a circle, all advance and retire twice. (8 bars)

(b) Ladies join right hands in the centre and dance around clockwise, then join left hands and dance back, passing in front of their own partners into their own places. (8 bars)

(c) Gents join right hands in the centre and dance around, then join left hands and dance back to place. On the way back, each gent places his right arm around the waist of the lady before his own and brings her on to his position. (8 bars)

(d) All swing their new partners in waltz hold. (8 bars)

(e) Each gent places his right arm around the lady's waist as she places her hand on his shoulder and all lead around clockwise, ladies on the inside. (8 bars)

(f) Repeat (b) to (e) until leading around with their own partners. (96 bars)

(g) All couples dance at home. (8 bars)

(h) Circle, advance and retire twice to finish. (8 bars)

(i) All swing in the circle, arms around backs ('big Christmas'). (8 bars)

FIGURE 5 : SLIP JIG

(a) All face their own partners, link right elbows and turn around each other twice, then chain around the set in this manner, turning once around each person they meet, alternating between right and left elbows. Gents move anticlockwise and ladies clockwise. All turn once with their partners when they get home. (32 bars)

(b) Top couple link right arms and turn once around each other, then, with the lady going to her right and the gent going to his left, each of them dances around all the other dancers in the set, turning once around each dancer as they go all round the set. Each time they turn around a dancer, they turn around each other in the centre before moving on to the next dancer. Only the first top dancers move on during this chain. The others only turn in place with the 'visitor' when they arrive. Finally, the top couple turn once around each other in place.

(c) Second top couple dance (b).

(d) First side couple dance (b).

(e) Second side couple dance (b).

(f) All repeat (a)

DONEGAL SET

This set was taught by Connie Ryan at his class in Churchtown in the late 1980s. A slightly different version was published by Comhaltas Ceoltóirí Éireann in their set-dancing book Coiscéim.

FIGURE 1: JIG (88 BARS)

(a) All couples house around in waltz hold. (8 bars)

(b) Top couples pass through, with each lady passing between the opposite couple, and pass right shoulder to right at the other side as gents cross outside the ladies to face in from opposite positions. They dance back to home, dancing into their own places in the same way. (8 bars)

(c) Top couples swing in place in waltz hold. (8 bars)

(d) Top couples repeat (b) and (c). (16 bars)

(e) Side couples dance (b) to (d). (32 bars)

(f) All couples house around in waltz hold. (8 bars)

FIGURE 2: POLKA (144 BARS)

(a) Top couples house around each other. (8 bars)

(b) Holding right hand in right, top couples advance and retire. As they retire, each gent brings his right arm back over his partner's head to rest it on her shoulder, then both couples lead anticlockwise to the opposite positions, where each gent brings his arm forward over the lady's head to hold hands in front again. (8 bars)

(c) Top couples repeat (b), leading back to their own positions. (8 bars)

(d) All couples swing in place. (8 bars)

(e) Repeat (a) to (d), with side couples dancing (a) to (c). (32 bars)

(f) Repeat (a) to (e), top couples and side couples leading again. (64 bars)

(g) All couples house around in waltz hold. (8 bars)

FIGURE 3: JIG (144 BARS)

(a) Top couples house around each other. (8 bars)

(b) Passing right shoulder to right, top gent and opposite lady dance clockwise around each other twice, to finish on their own side almost back in their own places. (8 bars)

(c) The top gent now takes the opposite lady's right hand in his left and his own partner's left hand in his right, while the opposite lady takes her partner's right hand in her left. All lead around anticlockwise in a line of four until they are back in their own positions. (8 bars)

(d) Top couples swing in place. (8 bars)

(e) Top couples repeat (a) to (d) with opposite couple leading. (32 bars)

(f) Side couples dance (a) to (e). First side couple are on the left of first top couple. (64 bars)

(g) All couples house around in waltz hold. (8 bars)

FIGURE 4: POLKA (240 BARS)

(a) Top ladies chain. They take right arms in the centre as they pass each other, then turn twice, left arm in left with the opposite gent and dance back to home, passing right shoulder to right in the centre. (8 bars)

(b) Top couples swing in place. (8 bars)

(c) As the second couple stand in place with the gent's arm over the lady's shoulder, right hand in right, first top couple house across to leave the lady beside the opposite gent, who places his left arm over her left shoulder, taking her left hand in his left. Top gent now takes the ladies' other hands as he faces the other three. (8 bars)

(d) The line of three advances and retires, then advances again, and the ladies turn, the top lady anticlockwise and the second lady clockwise, to stand beside the top gent, who has his arms over their shoulders, as the second gent now faces the line of three. (8 bars)

(e) The line of three advances and retires, then advances again, and the ladies turn in, the top lady clockwise and the second lady anticlockwise, to form a circle of four in the centre. (8 bars)

(f) With the ladies' hands resting on the gents' shoulders, the top couples swing clockwise in four in the centre (8 bars), then swing anticlockwise (6 bars) and break back to their own places (2 bars).(16 bars)

(g) Top couples repeat (a) to (f), with second couple leading. (56 bars)

(h) Side couples dance (a) to (g). First side couple are on the left of first top couple. (112 bars)

(i) All couples house around in waltz hold. (8 bars)

FIGURE 5: SINGLE REEL (152 BARS)

(a) All advance and retire twice in a circle. (8 bars)

(b) All couples swing in place. (8 bars)

(c) All lead around, with the gent's arm around his partner's waist. During the last two bars, each lady moves on, passing behind

(outside) the next gent on the right to stand in the lady's position
beside him. (8 bars)

(d) Repeat (a) to (c) until all are leading around with their own
partners again. This time the ladies do not move on – they stay
with their own partners, taking waltz hold. (96 bars)

(e) All advance and retire twice in a circle. (8 bars)

(f) All couples swing in place. (8 bars)

(g) All couples house around in waltz hold. (8 bars)

DROMGARRIFF HALF SET

This half-set from County Limerick is written as described by Miley Costello. My thanks to Eileen O'Doherty for notes and details.

FIGURE 1: JIG (112 BARS)

(a) Both couples dance four bars in waltz hold, dancing in and back twice, then house across to opposite positions. (8 bars)

(b) Both couples dance four bars in place, then house back to home positions. (8 bars)

(c) Holding their partner's right hand in their right, both couples lead anticlockwise around the set, stopping to turn the lady clockwise in each position. (16 bars)

(d) Both couples advance and retire once, then pass through to opposite positions. Top couple pass inside second couple and all turn in at the other side to face back, with gents in the ladies' positions. (8 bars)

(e) Repeat (d), dancing back to place. (8 bars)

(f) Both couples swing in waltz hold. (8 bars)

(g) Ladies chain with right hands in the centre, turn with left hand around opposite gent and pass back right shoulder to right. (8 bars)

(h) Both couples house around each other. (8 bars)

(i) Both couples dance four bars in place, then house across to opposite positions. (8 bars)

(j) Both couples dance four bars in place, then house back to home positions. (8 bars)

(k) Holding their partner's right hand in their right, both couples lead anticlockwise around the set, stopping to turn the lady clockwise in each position. (16 bars)

FIGURE 2: JIG (112 BARS)

(a) Both couples dance four bars in place, then house across to opposite positions. (8 bars)

(b) Both couples dance four bars in place, then house back to home positions. (8 bars)

(c) Both couples lead around anticlockwise, each lady crossing in front of the gent to home and turning anticlockwise under his right hand as he dances clockwise around her, passing through her position to his own. (8 bars)

(d) Both couples house around each other. (8 bars)

(e) Both couples square: slide to the position on the right, reverse into opposite position and house back to place. (8 bars)

(f) All advance and retire once holding right hand in right, then ladies cross to join the opposite gent. (8 bars)

(g) All house with new partners. (8 bars)

(h) All square the house, as in (e), with their new partners. (8 bars)

(i) Both couples advance and retire once, then ladies chain with their right hands in the centre and turn with their left hands around their original partner into their original place. (8 bars)

(j) Ladies dance a full chain, taking right hands in the centre, turning with left hands around the opposite gent, and taking right hands in the centre as they dance back to place. (8 bars)

(k) Both couples house around each other. (8 bars)

(l) Both couples dance four bars in place, then house across to opposite positions. (8 bars)

(m) Both couples dance four bars in place, then house back to home positions. (8 bars)

FIGURE 3: HORNPIPE (112 BARS)

(a) Both couples dance the body. In waltz hold, they dance in (hop 1 2 3) and back (hop 1 2 3), then turn clockwise to the next position on their right and repeat these movements three times, dancing around the set to home. (16 bars)

(b) Both couples dance around the house. (8 bars)

(c) Holding crossed hands, both couples dance to their left, facing out of the set, then reverse to the opposite position. (8 bars)

(d) Ladies chain, taking right arms in the centre and turning twice around each other to finish facing the opposite gent. While the ladies are chaining, the gents turn slowly anticlockwise in place. (8 bars)

(e) All dance the body as in (a) with new partners. (16 bars)

(f) All house with new partners. (8 bars)

(g) Both couples dance to their left, facing out of the set (4 bars), then reverse to the opposite position (4 bars). (8 bars)

(h) Ladies chain, taking right arms in the centre and turning twice around each other to finish facing opposite gent. While the ladies are chaining, the gents turn slowly anticlockwise in place. (8 bars)

(i) Both couples dance the body. In waltz hold, they dance in (hop 1 2 3) and back (hop 1 2 3), then turn clockwise to the next position on their right and repeat these movements three times, dancing around the set to home. (16 bars)

(j) Both couples dance around the house. (8 bars)

EAST GALWAY REEL SET

(SHORT VERSION)

This version of the set was taught by Connie Ryan at the Malahide Workshop. I received additional advice and information on it from Paul Moran.

FIGURE 1 : REEL (56 bars)

(a) All couples, holding crossed hands, square around the house. They dance forward to the next position on their right (2 bars), dance to the next position with the gent reversing and the lady going forward (2 bars), dance forward to the third position (2 bars) and dance to home with the gent reversing and the lady going forward again (2 bars). (8 bars)

(b) In half-sets, each top couple and the side couple on their left (who face them before starting the square) dance the 'ducks'. The two ladies dance clockwise around in the space between the two couples, each followed by her own partner, in a circle of four. During the last two bars, all dancers turn clockwise as they move into their own places, gents passing outside their own partners into place. (8 bars)

(c) All couples swing in *céilí* hold. (8 bars)

(d) Repeat (a) to (c). (24 bars)

FIGURE 2 : REEL (72 BARS)

(a) All couples square around the house. (8 bars)

(b) All advance and retire in half-sets, then square to the other couple's position. All advance and retire in half-sets, then square back to home. (16 bars)

(c) All couples swing. (8 bars)

(d) Repeat (a) to (c). (32 bars)

FIGURE 3 : REEL (88 BARS)

(a) All couples square around the house. (8 bars)

(b) All advance and retire in half-sets, then square to the other couple's position. All advance and retire in half-sets, then square back to home. (16 bars)

(c) All couples square around the house. (8 bars)

(d) All couples swing. (8 bars)

(e) Repeat (a) to (d). (40 bars)

FIGURE 4 : JIG (88 BARS)

(a) All couples square around the house. (8 bars)

(b) All advance and retire in half-sets, then turn clockwise once in place, holding crossed hands all the time. (8 bars)

(c) All couples advance and retire again, then turn anticlockwise once in place, holding crossed hands all the time. (8 bars)

(d) All couples square around the house. (8 bars)

(e) All couples swing. (8 bars)

(f) Repeat (a) to (e). (40 bars)

FIGURE 5 : REEL (104 BARS)

(a) All couples square around the house. (8 bars)

(b) In half-sets, all advance and retire. Then ladies change places, passing right shoulder to right and turning clockwise as they cross to face the opposite gent. They turn around one and a half times as they cross, while the gents turn clockwise in place. (8 bars)

(c) All swing with new partners. (8 bars)

(d) Repeat (b), with ladies going back to their own partners. (8 bars)

(e) All house around with their own partners. (8 bars)

(f) All couples swing. (8 bars)

(g) Repeat (a) to (f), sometimes swinging in four or eight at (f). (48 bars)

EAST GALWAY REEL SET

(LONG VERSION)

As taught by Seamus Ó Méalóid. This set is danced around the Aughrim and Kilconnell areas of east County Galway.

FIGURE 1: REEL (96 BARS)

(a) Body: All couples face partners, holding crossed hands. While side couples turn once in place, top couples cross, dancing a half-turn clockwise to opposite positions (2 bars), then all dance battering steps in place, facing their partners all the time (2 bars). Next, side couples cross while top couples turn in place and all dance the batter again (4 bars). All now repeat the movements, crossing back to their own positions. (16 bars)

(b) Figure: Top couples face left and side couples face right. With each lady dancing in front of her partner, each group of four dance one full clockwise circle, to finish back in their own places. Each gent dances outside his partner, right shoulder to right, as they turn clockwise to face each other in place. (8 bars)

(c) All couples swing in *céilí* hold. (8 bars)

(d) Repeat (a) to (c) with side couples leading. (32 bars)

(e) All couples dance the long house: holding crossed hands, they turn once to the position on the right (2 bars) and dance the batter there, facing their partners (2 bars). They then repeat the turn and batter as they move on to each position, dancing around the set to home positions (12 bars). (16 bars)

(f) All couples swing in place. (8 bars)

FIGURE 2: REEL (112 BARS)

(a) All couples dance the body, as in Figure 1. (16 bars)

(b) Figure: Top couples turn left and side couples turn right. Facing their own partners holding crossed hands, all advance, retire, and turn clockwise as they change places with the other couple (8 bars). All advance and retire again, then dance back to home.(16 bars)

(c) All couples swing in place. (8 bars)

(d) Repeat (a) to (c) with side couples leading. (40 bars)

(e) All couples dance the long house, as in Figure 1. (16 bars)

(f) All couples swing in place. (8 bars)

FIGURE 3: REEL (112 BARS)

(a) All couples dance the body, as in Figure 1.   (16 bars)

(b) All couples advance, facing partners with crossed hands, dance the batter, retire and dance the batter again.   (8 bars)

(c) All couples dance around to opposite positions (2 bars), dance the batter (2 bars), dance around to home (2 bars) and dance the batter again (2 bars).   (8 bars)

(d) All couples swing in place.   (8 bars)

(e) Repeat (a) to (d) with side couples leading.   (40 bars)

(f) All couples dance the long house, as in Figure 1.   (16 bars)

(g) All couples swing in place.   (8 bars)

FIGURE 4: JIG (128 BARS)

(a) All couples dance the body, as in Figure 1.   (16 bars)

(b) Top couples turn left and side couples turn right. Facing partners, holding crossed hands, all advance and retire, then turn once clockwise in place.   (8 bars)

(c) All couples advance and retire again, then turn anticlockwise once in place.   (8 bars)

(d) All couples dance, turning clockwise to opposite positions, dance the batter, dance around to home and dance the batter again.   (8 bars)

(e) All couples swing in place.   (8 bars)

(f) All repeat (a) to (e) with side couples leading.   (48 bars)

(g) All couples dance the long house, as in Figure 1.   (16 bars)

(h) All couples swing in place.   (8 bars)

FIGURE 5: REEL (160 BARS)

(a) All couples dance the body, as in Figure 1.   (16 bars)

(b) Top couples turn left and side couples turn right. All advance and retire once, facing partners with crossed hands, then ladies change places while gents turn clockwise once in place.   (8 bars)

(c) All swing their new partners.   (8 bars)

(d) Repeat (a) to (c) with side couples leading. (Side couples turn left at (b).)   (32 bars)

(e) Repeat (a) to (d), top couples and side couples leading again.   (64 bars)

(f) All couples dance the long house.   (16 bars)

(g) All swing in a circle of eight to finish the set.   (8 bars)

GLENCORRIB SET

(SOUTH MAYO)

This set has been danced in the Glencorrib area for generations. I first heard about it from Matt Cunningham, who recorded music for it during Easter 1999. Written notes on the set were provided by Bridget 'Del' May of Glencorrib.

FIGURE 1: JIG (72 BARS)

(a) All couples advance and retire twice holding crossed hands.　　(8 bars)

(b) All couples swing in place in *céilí* hold.　　(8 bars)

(c) Top couples advance and retire once, then cross on the left to the opposite side, with each lady turning clockwise once under her partner's hands.　　(8 bars)

(d) Top couples advance and retire once, then cross on the left to home, with each lady turning anticlockwise once under her partner's hands.　　(8 bars)

(e) Top couples swing in place in *céilí* hold.　　(8 bars)

(f) Side couples dance (c) and (d).　　(16 bars)

(g) All couples swing in place in *céilí* hold.　　(8 bars)

FIGURE 2: JIG (88 BARS)

(a) All couples advance and retire twice holding crossed hands.　　(8 bars)

(b) All couples swing in place in *céilí* hold.　　(8 bars)

(c) Top couples advance and retire twice.　　(8 bars)

(d) Top ladies link right arms in the centre and dance one full turn around each other, then turn with left hand under the opposite gent's left arm as they dance anticlockwise around him to the opposite lady's position. The gent does not turn.　　(8 bars)

(e) Top ladies link right arms in the centre and dance one full turn around each other, then turn clockwise, with left hand under their own partner's left arm, to finish on his left-hand side.　　(8 bars)

(f) Top couples swing in place in *céilí* hold, starting the swing in their partner's position and finishing in their own.　　(8 bars)

(g) Side couples dance (c) to (e).　　(24 bars

(h) All couples swing in place in *céilí* hold.　　(8 bars)

Figure 3: Jig (120 bars)

(a) All couples advance and retire twice holding crossed hands. (8 bars)

(b) All couples swing in place in *céilí* hold. (8 bars)

(c) Top couples advance and retire twice. (8 bars)

(d) Top ladies link right arms in the centre and dance one full turn around each other, then turn clockwise, with left hand under the opposite gent's left arm, to finish on his left-hand side. (8 bars)

(e) Top ladies swing opposite gents, ladies starting in the gent's position and finishing in the lady's position. (8 bars)

(f) Gents place their left arm around the new lady's waist as she places her right hand on his shoulder and both couples lead around clockwise. (8 bars)

(g) Top ladies link right arms in the centre and dance one full turn around each other, then turn clockwise, with left hand under their own partner's left arm, to finish on his left-hand side. (8 bars)

(h) Top couples swing in place in *céilí* hold, starting the swing in their partner's position and finishing in their own. (8 bars)

(i) Side couples dance (c) to (g). (40 bars)

(j) All couples swing in place in *céilí* hold. (8 bars)

Figure 4: Jig (104 bars)

(a) All couples advance and retire twice holding crossed hands. (8 bars)

(b) All couples swing in place in *céilí* hold. (8 bars)

(c) Top couples advance and retire twice. (8 bars)

(d) Holding right hand in right, first top couple advance to face opposite couple in the centre (2 bars). Second gent takes top lady's left hand in left and all retire, ladies going with the second gent (2 bars). Both ladies turn in under second gent's arms as the gents dance on the spot (2 bars), then all four advance to the centre again (2 bars). (8 bars)

(e) Top gent now takes the ladies' free hands and both gents retire, the ladies going with the top gent (2 bars). Both ladies turn in under the top gent's arms as the gents dance on the spot (2 bars), then all advance to form a basket in the centre (2 bars) and ladies turn out to place their hands on the gents' shoulders (2 bars). (8 bars)

(f) Top couples swing in a basket in the centre. (8 bars)

(g) Side couples dance (c) to (f). First side couple are on the right. (32 bars)

(h) All couples advance and retire twice holding crossed hands. (8 bars)

(i) All couples swing in place in *céilí* hold. (8 bars)

FIGURE 5: POLKA (88 BARS)

(a) All couples slide to the centre and back twice in waltz hold. (8 bars)

(b) All couples swing in place in waltz hold. (8 bars)

(c) Top couples slide to the centre and back twice in waltz hold. (8 bars)

(d) Top couples pass through to opposite positions, with first top couple in the centre, and turn in on the spot at the other side to face back. The gents are now in the opposite ladies' positions while the ladies are in the opposite gents' positions. (8 bars)

(e) Top couples pass back to home positions, with second top couple in the centre, and turn on the spot to face their partners in their own places. (8 bars)

(f) All couples swing in place in waltz hold. (8 bars)

(g) Side couples dance (c) to (e). (24 bars)

(h) All couples swing in place in waltz hold. (8 bars)

FIGURE 6: POLKA (136 BARS)

(a) All couples slide to the centre and back twice in waltz hold. (8 bars)

(b) All couples swing in place in waltz hold. (8 bars)

(c) Top couples slide to the centre and back twice in waltz hold. (8 bars)

(d) Top ladies change places, passing right shoulder to right, dancing two bars in the centre. (8 bars)

(e) Top gents change places, passing left shoulder to left, dancing two bars in the centre. (8 bars)

(f) Top ladies change back to their own places, passing right shoulder to right, dancing two bars in the centre. (8 bars)

(g) Top gents change back to their own places, passing left shoulder to left, dancing two bars in the centre. (8 bars)

(h) All couples swing in place in waltz hold. (8 bars)

(i) Side couples dance (c) to (g). (40 bars)

(j) All couples swing in place in waltz hold. (8 bars)

(k) All couples slide to the centre and back twice in waltz hold. (8 bars)

(l) All couples swing in place in waltz hold. (8 bars)

GLENCREE SET

The source of this polka set, Bill Quinn of Glencree, County Wicklow, was contacted by Daithí Ó hÓgáin and put in touch with Connie Ryan. It is a quadrille set, similar to the Kilkenny Quadrilles and others danced throughout south and east Leinster.

FIGURE 1: POLKA (136 BARS)

(a) Top couples cross to the other side, each lady passing between the opposite couple and gents passing on the outside. All turn clockwise at the opposite side and pass back. Each lady, right hand in right, turns anticlockwise under her partner's arm into place.   (8 bars)

(b) Top couples now take right hand in right and left hand in left and dance anticlockwise around inside, each lady in front of her partner. As they move around, ladies turn right (1 bar) and left (1 bar) four times, continuing the last left (anticlockwise) turn to bring hands down in front as they arrive back in place.   (8 bars)

(c) Top ladies chain, linking right arms in the centre and left arm to the opposite gent, and dance back to turn anticlockwise, right hand in right under their partner's arm into place.   (8 bars)

(d) Top couples swing in *céilí* hold.   (8 bars)

(e) Side couples dance (a) to (d).   (32 bars)

(f) Repeat (a) to (e), all couples swinging at (d) the last time.   (64 bars)

FIGURE 2: POLKA (168 BARS)

(a) Top ladies chain, as in Figure 1 (c).   (8 bars)

(b) Top couples advance and retire twice holding crossed hands. As they retire the second time, ladies turn anticlockwise under the gent's right arm only, then take both hands again and cross anticlockwise to opposite positions, with ladies turning right and left twice in front of the gents, as in Figure 1 (b).   (12 bars)

(c) Repeat (b) in opposite positions, crossing back to home.   (12 bars)

(d) Top couples swing in *céilí* hold.   (8 bars)

(e) Side couples dance (a) to (d).   (40 bars)

(f) Repeat (a) to (e), all couples swinging at (d) the last time.   (80 bars)

FIGURE 3: POLKA (168 BARS)

(a) Top ladies chain, as in Figure 1 (c).   (8 bars)

(b) Top gents cross (2 bars) and swing opposite lady (6 bars).   (8 bars)

(c) Top gents hook left arms in the centre, dance one and a half turns, then take their partner's right hand in their right, and ladies turn anticlockwise under their arm as they cross to home, taking both hands.   (8 bars)

(d) Top couples dance around inside anticlockwise, ladies turning, as in Figure 1 (b).   (8 bars)

(e) Top couples swing in *céilí* hold.   (8 bars)

(f) Side couples dance (a) to (e).   (40 bars)

(g) Repeat (a) to (f), all couples swinging at (e) the last time.   (80 bars)

FIGURE 4: POLKA (168 BARS)

(a) Top ladies chain, as in Figure 1 (c).   (8 bars)

(b) From the chain, the second top lady stays facing out of the set, holding her partner's right hand. First top couple swing, moving across the set to leave the lady facing out of the set, beside the second gent, who now holds both ladies' hands as they face him.   (8 bars)

(c) As the first top gent retires to stay in place, the line of three crosses, the gent going forward as the ladies reverse, then crosses back to the second position, ladies going forward as the gent reverses. Now all four advance to the centre (2 bars), ladies giving their free hands (underneath) to the lone gent and turning under the gents' arms as he pulls them towards him to form a circle of four, with arms around each other's backs.   (8 bars)

(d) Top couples swing in four in the centre.   (8 bars)

(e) Top couples repeat (a) to (d), with second couple swinging at (b).(32 bars)

(f) Top ladies chain again.   (8 bars)

(g) Top couples swing in *céilí* hold.   (8 bars)

(h) Side couples dance (a) to (g), all couples swinging at (g).   (80 bars)

FIGURE 6: JIG (136 BARS)

(a) Top ladies chain, as in Figure 1(c).   (8 bars)

(b) In waltz hold, top couples dance one step in and one step back twice (4 bars), then gallop across and back, gents passing back to back both times (4 bars).   (8 bars)

(c) Top ladies chain, as in (a).   (8 bars)

(d) Top couples swing in *céilí* hold.   (8 bars)

(e) Side couples dance (a) to (d).   (32 bars)

(f) Repeat (a) to (e), all couples swinging at (e) the last time.   (64 bars)

FIGURE 6: WALTZ

(a) All advance and retire twice in a circle.   (8 bars)

(b) Gents waltz with the lady on their left, dancing two clockwise turns with her as they move back to the lady's position, then dance anticlockwise there, turning twice.   (16 bars)

(c) Repeat (a) and (b) until back at home, all with their own partners. (72 bars)

(d) All join in a general waltz.

GLENGARRIFF POLKA SET

(SHORT VERSION)

As described by local dancers to Olive Lynch of Bantry, County Cork.

FIGURE 1 (PASS THROUGH): POLKA (96 BARS)

(a) All advance and retire twice in a circle.   (8 bars)

(b) Top couples slide to the centre (1 2, 1 2) and back, then dance one turn in place.   (8 bars)

(c) Top couples pass through – the first couple take right hand in right and pass through the centre, while the second couple move apart to cross on the outside, gent on his left and lady on her right (4 bars). At the other side all turn in towards their partners and cross back, with second couple passing through the centre and top couple on the outside (4 bars).   (8 bars)

(d) All couples dance the body – dance in (1 2 3), on (1 2 3), then turn clockwise to the position on their right. They repeat this three times, all dancing around the set to home.   (16 bars)

(e) All couples dance around the house.   (8 bars)

(f) Repeat (b) to (e) with side couples dancing (b) and (c).   (40 bars)

FIGURE 2 (DOUBLE POLKA): POLKA (96 BARS)

(a) All advance and retire twice in a circle.   (8 bars)

(b) Top couples slide to the centre and back, then dance at home.   (8 bars)

(c) Top ladies chain with right hands in the centre, left hands around opposite gent, right hands again and swing their partners once in waltz hold.   (8 bars)

(d) All couples dance in and back twice (4 bars) and house across to opposite positions.   (8 bars)

(e) All couples repeat (d), dancing around to home.   (8 bars)

(f) All couples dance around the house.   (8 bars)

(g) Repeat (b) to (f) with side couples dancing (b) and (c) .   (40 bars)

FIGURE 3 (DOUBLE SLIDE): POLKA (96 BARS)

(a) All advance and retire twice in a circle.   (8 bars)

(b) Top couples slide to the centre and back, then dance at home.   (8 bars)

(c) Top couples repeat (b).   (8 bars)

(d) All couples slide to the centre and back, then house around to opposite positions. (8 bars)

(e) All couples repeat (d), dancing around to home. (8 bars)

(f) All couples dance around the house. (8 bars)

(e) Repeat (b) to (f), with side couples dancing (b) and (c). (40 bars)

FIGURE 4 : POLKA (160 BARS)

(a) All advance and retire twice in a circle. (8 bars)

(b) Top couples house around each other. (8 bars)

(c) Top couples slide to the centre and back, then house around to opposite positions. (8 bars)

(d) All couples repeat (c), dancing around to home. (8 bars)

(e) Top couples house around each other. (8 bars)

(f) Top couples advance and retire, with the gent's arm around the lady's waist and her hand on his shoulder (4 bars), then ladies cross right shoulder to right (2 bars) and swing one turn with the opposite gent (2 bars). (8 bars)

(g) Top couples repeat (f), with the ladies crossing back to home. (8 bars)

(h) All couples dance in and back twice (4 bars) and house across to opposite positions. (8 bars)

(i) All couples repeat (h), dancing around to home. (8 bars)

(j) All couples dance around the house. (8 bars)

(k) Repeat (b) to (j) with side couples dancing (b) to (g). (72 bars)

FIGURE 5 : POLKA (208 BARS)

(a) All advance and retire twice in a circle. (8 bars)

(b) First top couple 'show the lady'. (8 bars)

(c) First top couple slide to the centre and back, then dance at home. (8 bars)

(d) Ladies move on and swing the gent on the right. (8 bars)

(e) All couples dance the body, as in Figure 1, then house around. (24 bars)

(f) Repeat (b) to (e) three times, each gent leading in turn and ladies dancing with each gent as they move around the set. First side couple are on the right of first top couple. (144 bars)

GLENGARRIFF POLKA SET

(LONG VERSION)

*As described by local dancers to Olive Lynch
of Bantry, County Cork.*

FIGURE 1 (PASS THROUGH): POLKA (176 BARS)

(a) All advance and retire twice in a circle. (8 bars)

(b) First top couple house inside ('show the lady'). (8 bars)

(c) First top couple slide to the centre (1 2, 1 2) and back, then dance
one turn in place. (8 bars)

(d) All couples dance the body – dance in (1 2 3), on (1 2 3), then turn
clockwise to the position on their right. They repeat this three
times, all dancing around the set to home positions. (16 bars)

(e) All couples dance around the house. (8 bars)

(f) Repeat (b) to (e) with first side couple (on the left), second top
couple and second side couple leading in turn. (120 bars)

FIGURE 2 (DOUBLE POLKA): POLKA (208 BARS)

(a) All advance and retire twice in a circle. (8 bars)

(b) First top couple house inside ('show the lady'). (8 bars)

(c) First top couple slide to the centre (1 2, 1 2) and back, then dance
one turn in place. (8 bars)

(d) Top ladies chain with right hands in the centre, left hands around
opposite gent, right hands again and swing their partners once in
waltz hold. (8 bars)

(e) All couples dance in and back twice (4 bars) and house across to
opposite positions. (8 bars)

(f) All couples repeat (d), dancing around to home. (8 bars)

(g) All couples dance around the house. (8 bars)

(h) Repeat (b) to (g) with first side couple (on the left), second top
couple and second side couple leading in turn. (144 bars)

FIGURE 3 (DOUBLE SLIDE): POLKA (176 BARS)

(a) All advance and retire twice in a circle. (8 bars)

(b) First top couple house inside ('show the lady'). (8 bars)

(c) First top couple slide to the centre (1 2, 1 2) and back, then dance
one turn in place. (8 bars)

(d) All couples slide to the centre and back, then house around to
    opposite positions. (8 bars)

(e) All couples repeat (d), dancing around to home. (8 bars)

(f) All couples dance around the house. (8 bars)

(e) Repeat (b) to (f) with first side couple (on the left), second top
    couple and second side couple leading in turn. (120 bars)

FIGURE 4 : POLKA (160 BARS)

(a) All advance and retire twice in a circle. (8 bars)

(b) Top couples house around each other. (8 bars)

(c) Top couples slide to the centre and back, then house around to
    opposite positions. (8 bars)

(d) All couples repeat (c), dancing around to home. (8 bars)

(e) Top couples house around each other. (8 bars)

(f) Top couples advance and retire with the gent's arm around the
    lady's waist and her hand on his shoulder (4 bars), then ladies
    cross right shoulder to right (2 bars) and swing one turn with the
    opposite gent (2 bars). (8 bars)

(g) Top couples repeat (f) with ladies crossing back home. (8 bars)

(h) All couples dance in and back twice (4 bars) and house across to
    opposite positions. (8 bars)

(i) All couples repeat (h), dancing around to home. (8 bars)

(j) All couples dance around the house. (8 bars)

(k) Repeat (b) to (j) with side couples dancing (b) to (g). (72 bars)

FIGURE 5 : POLKA (208 BARS)

(a) All advance and retire twice in a circle. (8 bars)

(b) First top couple 'show the lady'. (8 bars)

(c) First top couple slide to the centre and back, then dance at home.
    (8 bars)

(d) Ladies move on and swing the gent on the right. (8 bars)

(e) All couples dance the body, as in Figure 1, then house around. (24 bars)

(f) Repeat (b) to (e) three times, each gent leading in turn and ladies
    dancing with each gent as they move around the set. First side
    couple are on the left of first tops. (144 bars)

HOLLYMOUNT SET

This Mayo set was taught in Dublin by Margaret Geraghty of Hollymount in October 1999 at a workshop arranged by Eileen O'Doherty.

FIGURE 1: JIG (264 BARS)

(a) Holding crossed hands, all four couples advance, dance on the spot, retire and dance on the spot again.   (8 bars)

(b) As in the Newport Set, top couples dance to their left, dance on the spot facing the side couple, then reverse to opposite positions. When dancing to the left, the ladies move forward more than the gents, and when reversing to opposite positions, the gents retire more than the ladies.   (8 bars)

(c) Repeat (b) from opposite positions, dancing to the left again and reversing back to home.   (8 bars)

(d) Top couples swing (6 bars) and dance out facing into the set (2 bars).   (8 bars)

(e) Top ladies chain with right hands in the centre, turn clockwise under opposite gent's left arm while dancing anticlockwise around him (he does not turn), then pass right shoulder to right and turn clockwise to face into the set. During the last two bars, gents advance to stand beside their partners.   (8 bars)

(f) Top couples swing in four in the centre, ladies' hands resting on the gents' shoulders (6 bars), and reverse to place (2 bars).   (8 bars)

(g) Top couples repeat (b) and (c).   (16 bars)

(h) Side couples dance (b) to (g).   (56 bars)

(i) All dancers face clockwise around the set in single file. They dance to the first position left of their own (2 bars) and dance on the spot there (2 bars), then repeat the movements three times, dancing around the set to home (12 bars). During the last two bars, all gents turn clockwise to face their partners.   (16 bars)

(j) All couples swing (6 bars) and dance out facing into the set (2 bars).(8 bars)

(k) Top couple dance across holding right hands and top gent takes the opposite lady's left hand as his own partner turns to face him (4 bars). He reverses to place, ladies dancing forward, and brings his hands back onto the ladies' shoulders as they turn in beside him (4 bars).   (8 bars)

(l) Second top gent now crosses to face the line of three and each gent takes the opposite lady's right hand in his right (4 bars). The second gent retires with the first top lady and each lady dances clockwise into the opposite lady's position. (8 bars)

(m) Top couples swing new partners (6 bars) and dance out facing into the set (2 bars). (8 bars)

(n) Top couples repeat (k) to (m) with second top gent leading and ladies crossing back to their own places. (24 bars)

(o) Side couples dance (k) to (n). First side couple are on the left of first top couple. (48 bars)

(p) Holding crossed hands, all four couples advance, dance on the spot and dance on the spot again. (8 bars)

(q) All couples swing (6 bars) and dance out facing into the set (2 bars). (8 bars)

FIGURE 2: POLKA (184 BARS)

(a) All couples dance in to the centre (tap 1, tap 2, tap 1 2 3) and back, then turn clockwise twice as they dance to the next position on their right (8 bars). They then repeat the movements three times as they dance around to each position, ending at home. (32 bars)

(b) Top couples swing (6 bars) and dance out facing into the set (2 bars). (8 bars)

(c) Gates: Top couples dance forward into a line, first couple in the centre holding hands low, second couple moving apart to stand on the outside. All turn with the free hand (top gent's left, top lady's right) around the opposite person to face back home (4 bars), then each gent turns the opposite lady clockwise under his left arm as he dances back to his own place, bringing her into his partner's place. (8 bars)

(d) Top couples swing new partners (6 bars) and dance out facing into the set. (8 bars)

(e) Top couples repeat (c) with the second top gent and his new partner, the top lady, dancing forward into the centre of the line to begin. Each gent now turns his own partner back to her own position. (8 bars)

(f) Top couples swing (6 bars) and dance out facing into the set (2 bars). (8 bars)

(g) Side couples dance (c) to (f). (32 bars)

(h) The four ladies join right hands in the centre and dance one and a half clockwise turns around the set, to finish beside the opposite gent. (8 bars)

(i) All swing new partners (6 bars) and dance out facing into the set. (8 bars)

(j) The four ladies join right hands in the centre and dance one and a half clockwise turns around the set, to finish beside their own partners. (8 bars)

(k) All couples swing (6 bars) and dance out facing into the set (2 bars). (8 bars)

(l) All couples repeat (a) and (b) to finish.   (40 bars)

HURRY THE JUG

This eight-hand dance from County Limerick was made popular by dancing teacher Timmy MacCarthy. Although it is referred to as a set and has three figures, it is danced straight through as one dance, much like the eight-hand jig or similar céilí dances. It is danced to jigs. My thanks to Eileen O'Doherty, Anne O'Donnell and Maureen Culleton for helping me learn this dance.

INTRODUCTION

(a) All lead around anticlockwise, holding crossed hands, until back in their own places. (8 bars)

(b) All turn in place and lead around clockwise until back in their own places. (8 bars)

BODY

(a) Quarter-chain: All face their partners and take right hand in right. They pass their partner and chain around the person facing them in the corner with their left hands, then chain back to turn with their right hands around their partners into place. (8 bars)

(b) Crossover: With top gents crossing ahead of side gents, all gents pass the opposite gent left shoulder to left to turn anticlockwise, left hand in left, around the opposite lady into the lady's position (4 bars). From there, all gents give their right hand to the lady in the position on their left and turn clockwise into the gent's position beside her (4 bars). Top gents are now in side positions and side gents are in top positions. With top gents leading again, all gents cross left shoulder to left to turn anticlockwise, left hand in left, around the lady who is now opposite (4 bars), then give their right hands to their own partners and turn clockwise into their own places (4 bars). (16 bars)

(c) Return chain: Taking their partner's right hand in right, all chain halfway around the set, ladies going clockwise and gents going anticlockwise. When the partners meet again, they turn around each other and chain back to their own places, ladies going anticlockwise and gents clockwise. When the partners meet after the chain, they shake hands. (16 bars)

(d) Tilly: still holding right hands, partners dance around each other into their own places. Then, with top couples moving to their right and side couples moving to their left, top gent and side gent pass

89

back to back and the two couples form a circle of four and dance on the spot with ladies facing in and gents facing out (4 bars). Letting their partner's hand go, all now turn anticlockwise, with left hands around the other lady or gent, and, taking their own partner's right hand again, turn clockwise into their own places (4 bars). (8 bars)

(e) Gallop: all couples dance the gallop with the couple opposite them in the set – tops crossing over, then sides crossing over and tops crossing back first, followed by sides. Gents pass back to back crossing over and ladies pass back to back crossing back. The steps for the gallop, dancing sideways, are 1 2 3, hop on the way over. Side couples cross while top couples dance 1 2 3, 1 2 3 in place at the other side, and sides dance 1 2 3, 1 2 3 while tops cross back. Side couples have no time to dance 1 2 3, 1 2 3 after they cross back themselves. (8 bars)

(f) Top couples now dance the gallop with the couple on their left. They gallop over and dance on the spot, then gallop back and dance in their own places. Again, gents pass back to back when crossing over and ladies pass back to back when crossing back. (8 bars)

FIGURE 1

(a) Taking right hand in right, top couples advance and retire once, then ladies change places, crossing right shoulder to right, and gents change places, crossing left shoulder to left. (8 bars)

(b) Top couples repeat (a), crossing back to their own places. (8 bars)

(c) Side couples dance (a) and (b). (16 bars)

BODY

(a) All dance the body (a) to (f) again. (64 bars)

FIGURE 2

(a) Top gents turn around each other with right hands in the centre until facing the gent on the right of their own original positions, then turn with left hand in left around this gent (4 bars). They now cross to turn with right hands around the opposite side lady, who is on the left of their own places, and the two top gents then move in to face each other in the centre. (8 bars)

(b) Top gents swing with each other in *céilí* hold in the centre. (8 bars)

(c) Side gents repeat (a) and (b). (16 bars)

BODY

(a) All dance the body (a) to (f) again. (64 bars)

FIGURE 3

(a) Top couples take their partners' inside hands and second top couples make an arch. Both top couples cross to opposite positions, with first top couple passing under the arch. In opposite positions, all turn in towards their partners, take their other hand and cross back. This time the first top couple make the arch and the second top couple pass under it. (8 bars)

(b) Top couples house, holding crossed hands. (8 bars)

(c) Side couples dance (a) and (b). (8 bars)

BODY

(a) All dance the body (a) to (f) again. (64 bars)

FINISH

(a) All lead around anticlockwise until back in their own places, holding crossed hands. (8 bars)

(b) All turn in place and lead around clockwise until back in their own places. (8 bars)

(c) All couples swing in *céilí* hold. (8 bars)

Inis Meáin Set

This set, as danced by local set dancers, was recorded by dancing teacher Maureen Culleton of Ballyfin, County Laois, and her dancers during a trip to Inis Meáin.

Figure 1: Reel (240 bars)

(a) In half-sets, all lead around anticlockwise, each lady in front of her partner. (8 bars)

(b) All couples swing in *céilí* hold. (8 bars)

(c) All couples advance and retire holding crossed hands, then cross anticlockwise to the opposite side, with each lady turning clockwise under her partner's right arm. (8 bars)

(d) Repeat (c), crossing back home. (8 bars)

(e) All couples swing in *céilí* hold. (8 bars)

(f) Ladies chain as in the Connemara Set, taking right hands in the centre and dancing anticlockwise around the opposite gent while turning clockwise under his left arm. The gent turns anticlockwise with the lady, then turns clockwise to face his own partner as she returns. (8 bars)

(g) All couples swing in *céilí* hold. (8 bars)

(h) First gent and opposite lady dance past each other, passing left shoulder to left in the centre, and turn clockwise (4 bars), then swing (8 bars) and dance back to take crossed hands with their partners (4 bars). (16 bars)

(i) All couples advance and retire holding crossed hands, then cross anticlockwise to the opposite side, with each lady turning clockwise under her partner's right arm. (8 bars)

(j) Repeat (i), crossing back home. (8 bars)

(k) All couples swing in *céilí* hold. (8 bars)

(l) Repeat (h) to (k) with second gent and opposite lady leading. (40 bars)

(m) While second couple stand in place holding right hand in right, first couple swing across the set to leave the first lady facing the second gent, holding his left hand in her left. During the last bar, the second lady moves anticlockwise to face her partner so that the two ladies stand facing him, holding his hands. The first gent stands alone. (8 bars)

(n) All dance forward and back twice, with the ladies taking the short turn during the last two bars to stand beside the second gent and give their free hands to the first gent. The first lady turns anticlockwise and the second lady turns clockwise. All are now holding hands. (8 bars)

(o) All advance and retire twice again, ladies turning in to stand in a circle. (8 bars)

(p) Ladies place their hands on the gents' shoulders and all swing in four in the centre. (8 bars)

(q) Ladies chain, as in the Connemara Set, taking right hands in the centre and dancing anticlockwise around the opposite gent while turning clockwise under his left arm. The gent turns anticlockwise with the lady, then turns clockwise to face his own partner as she returns. (8 bars)

(r) All couples swing in *céilí* hold. (8 bars)

(s) Repeat (m) to (r) with second couple leading. (48 bars)

FIGURE 2: POLKA (280 BARS)

(a) Four couples dance together in this figure. All lead around, the gent's arm around the lady's waist and her hand on his shoulder. (8 bars)

(b) All couples swing in *céilí* hold. (8 bars)

(c) Keeping the arm on the shoulder or around the waist, top couples advance and retire, then side couples advance and retire. (8 bars)

(d) Top couples cross anticlockwise to face in on the other side, then side couples cross anticlockwise to face in on the other side. (8 bars)

(e) All repeat (c) and (d), crossing back to home. (16 bars)

(f) Top ladies chain, as in the first figure, with side ladies chaining two bars behind them. (8 bars)

(g) All couples swing in *céilí* hold. (8 bars)

(h) Ladies move on to the right, passing outside the next gent to lead around with him. (8 bars)

(i) All couples swing in *céilí* hold. (8 bars)

(i) Repeat (c) to (i) until ladies are back swinging their own partners. (192 bars)

INIS OIRR SET

This set was first given to me in 1997 by Máiréad Sharry, who now resides in the village of Lurgan on Inis Oirr. In 1999 Micheál Ó hAmhain made a video recording of the set with some island dancers, and some of them taught me it during the workshop weekend in May 1999. The first three figures, described here as danced around the country, are danced as one very long figure on the island. The three parts are danced in half-sets and the last part is danced in a full square set with top and side couples.

FIGURE 1: REEL (120 BARS)

(a) Ladies change places, passing right shoulder to right, then gents change places, passing left shoulder to left. Ladies change back and gents change back. (8 bars)

(b) All face their partners in their own places and dance out on the spot. (8 bars)

(c) All couples swing in *céilí* hold. (8 bars)

(d) Ladies chain, taking right hands in the centre, turn with left hand under the opposite gent's arm, chain back and turn under their partner's arm into place. (8 bars)

(e) All dance out, facing their partners in place. (8 bars)

(f) All couples swing in *céilí* hold. (8 bars)

(g) Holding crossed hands, both couples advance, and as they retire ladies cross in front of their partners to the left, turning clockwise under the gent's hands, and all cross to the opposite side. (8 bars)

(h) Repeat (g), dancing back to home. (8 bars)

(i) All dance out, facing their partners in place. (8 bars)

(j) All couples swing in *céilí* hold. (8 bars)

(k) Holding crossed hands, both couples advance, and as they retire ladies cross in front of their partners to the left, turning clockwise under the gent's hands, and all cross to the opposite side. (8 bars)

(l) Repeat (k), dancing back to home. (8 bars)

(m) All dance out, facing their partners in place. (8 bars)

(n) All couples swing in *céilí* hold. (8 bars)

FIGURE 2: REEL (160 BARS)

(a) Ladies chain, taking right hands in the centre, turn with left hand under the opposite gent's arm, chain back and turn under their partner's arm into place. (8 bars)

(b) All dance out, facing their partners in place. (8 bars)

(c) All couples swing in *céilí* hold. (8 bars)

(d) Facing each other all the time, top lady and second gent dance all around each other, crossing right shoulder to right to opposite positions and back to face each other in the centre. (8 bars)

(e) Top lady and opposite gent swing in the centre (6 bars) and reverse back into their own places (2 bars). (8 bars)

(f) Holding crossed hands, both couples advance, and as they retire ladies cross in front of their partners to the left, turning clockwise under the gent's hands, and all cross to the opposite side. (8 bars)

(g) Top lady and second gent repeat (d) and (e), then all repeat (f), dancing back to home. (24 bars)

(h) All dance out, facing their partners in place. (8 bars)

(i) All couples swing in *céilí* hold. (8 bars)

(j) Repeat (d) to (i), with top gent and second lady leading. (64 bars)

FIGURE 3: REEL (160 BARS)

(a) Ladies chain, taking right hands in the centre, turn with left hand under the opposite gent's arm, chain back and turn under their partner's arm into place. (8 bars)

(b) All dance out, facing their partners in place. (8 bars)

(c) All couples swing in *céilí* hold. (8 bars)

(d) First couple house across in waltz hold to leave the lady beside the opposite gent, who holds the two ladies' hands as they face him. (8 bars)

(e) The line of three advances (4 bars) and retires, ladies turning to stand beside the second gent and giving their free hands to the top gent (4 bars). All now hold hands. (8 bars)

(f) The line of three advances as the top gent retires (4 bars). The line then retires, and ladies turn to form a circle of four in the centre, with the ladies' hands on the gents' shoulders (4 bars). (8 bars)

(g) The two couples swing in four in the centre, turning clockwise (8 bars), then anticlockwise (8 bars). (16 bars)

(h) Ladies chain, dance out and swing. (24 bars)

(i) Repeat (d) to (h) with second couple leading. (64 bars)

FIGURE 4: POLKA (136 BARS)

(a) All four couples hold hands in a circle, then advance and retire twice. (8 bars)

(b) All couples dance at home with their own partners. (8 bars)

(c) All advance and retire twice in the circle again, ladies moving

forward on the inside to the next gent on the right. She faces him
as she moves on to take waltz hold with him. (8 bars)

(d) All couples dance at home with their new partners. (8 bars)

(e) Repeat (c) and (d) until all the ladies move all round the set and
are back dancing in place with their own partners again. (48 bars)

(f) With side couples starting two bars behind top couples, all
couples advance and retire, then cross on the right in waltz hold
to opposite positions. They then advance, retire, cross back home
and dance one turn in place. (24 bars)

(g) Top ladies chain, followed by side ladies. They dance the usual
chain. (8 bars)

(h) All dance out (8 bars) and swing their partners to finish (8 bars). (16 bars)

Inverness South Square Set

(Cape Breton Island)

I first saw a version of this set at a party in Andy Cooper's house in Halifax, Nova Scotia, during Easter 1996. The following is based on notes given to me by Elizabeth MacDonald and Diane Milligan of Dans Nova Scotia in Halifax. As the terminology used in Cape Breton dance-calling is different to what we use in set dancing, I have adapted the notes here to suit set dancers. The set can be danced with almost any number of couples, but it is written here as danced with four couples. Variations are danced from place to place. During the introduction to each figure, all dancers acknowledge their partners and their corner person, who is on their other side.

Figure 1: Jig (144 bars)

(a) All advance and retire twice in a circle, dancing battering steps. (8 bars)

(b) Top couples face the side couple on the right. All dancers take both hands (right hand in left) with the opposite lady or gent. They advance towards each other (1 bar) and, circling clockwise, reverse into opposite (i.e. each other's) position (1 bar), then advance again and circle back to their own positions (2 bars). These movements are danced a second time (4 bars). (8 bars)

(c) Pass-through: Top couples face the side couple on their right again and pass through, each top couple holding hands as they pass between the side couple, who cross on the outside (4 bars). Top couples now move sideways to the outside and reverse back to place without turning, while side couples move sideways to take hands and reverse back in the centre. (8 bars)

(d) All turn from their partners to dance in place in the corner with the person on the other side. They either dance in waltz hold together or hold hands and step-dance. (8 bars)

(e) All advance and retire twice in a circle again. (8 bars)

(f) Top couples turn to face the couple on their left and repeat (b), all dancers circling clockwise twice around the opposite lady or gent. (8 bars)

(g) Top couples face the side couple on the left again and all dance the pass through, with top couples crossing over on the inside and reversing back on the outside. (8 bars)

(h) All dancers turn away from their partners to dance in the corner with the person on the other side. (8 bars)

(i) Repeat (a) to (h) with side couples leading. They cross over through the centre and reverse back on the outside at (c) and (g). (64 bars)

(j) All advance and retire twice in a circle to finish. (8 bars)

FIGURE 2: JIG (144 BARS)

(a) All advance and retire twice in a circle. (8 bars)

(b) The four ladies join right hands in a star in the centre and dance halfway around (4 bars), then join left hands and dance back to place. At the same time, the four gents dance to the right around the outside (4 bars), then turn and dance back to place. (8 bars)

(c) All couples dance in place. (8 bars)

(d) All couples promenade (lead around) to the right, each gent's arm around his partner's waist and her left hand on his right shoulder.

(8 bars)

(e) Repeat (a) to (c). (24 bars)

(f) All couples promenade (lead around), going to the left this time, ladies on the inside. (8 bars)

(g) Repeat (a) to (f). (64 bars)

(h) All advance and retire twice in a circle to finish. (8 bars)

FIGURE 3: REEL (296 BARS)

(a) Half grand chain: Taking their partner's right hand in their right, all chain to the opposite positions, ladies going clockwise and gents anticlockwise. (8 bars)

(b) All couples swing in opposite positions. (8 bars)

(c) All chain back to place, going back the way they came over, gents going clockwise and ladies anticlockwise this time. (8 bars)

(d) All couples promenade to the right, leading around to finish in a line-up facing the music. The first top couple are first in line, the first side couple (on the right of the first top couple) are second, the second side couple are third and the second top couple are fourth, with each lady on the right of her partner. (8 bars)

(e) First top couple turn in (lady anticlockwise and gent clockwise) to face the back, taking nearest hands. They lead down the centre, passing through the other couples, who turn in to follow them. At the end of the line, ladies turn left, gents turn right, and they dance or walk up on the outside to form two lines, with the ladies facing the gents. (8 bars)

(f) All 'show their steps' or 'step it off' – advance and retire four times (at least!) dancing battering steps. The steps can be quite varied, depending on the dancer's ability. (16 bars)

(g) All couples dance back to their own positions and dance in place. (8 bars)

(h) Repeat (a) to (g) with the second top couple leading the line-up at (d). They face out of their own position, the second side couple (on the right of the first top couple) are second in line, the first side couple are third and the first top couple are fourth. (64 bars)

(i) Repeat (a) to (h) with the first top couple leading the third time and the second top couple leading the fourth time. (128 bars)

(j) Full grand chain: Chain all the way around. (16 bars)

(k) Promenade (lead around) again. (8 bars)

(l) All advance and retire twice in a circle. (8 bars)

KILDOWNET HALF SET

This half-set comes from Achill Island, County Mayo. It was revived by dancing teacher Eamonn Gannon. The three figures are traditionally followed by a fling.

FIGURE 1: REEL (112 BARS)

(a) Holding both hands, both couples advance and retire twice.

(8 bars)

(b) Both couples square – dance to face to the position on their left, reverse into the position opposite their own, dance to face to their left again and reverse back to their own positions. (8 bars)

(c) Both couples swing in *céilí* hold. (8 bars)

(d) Ladies chain – right arms in the centre, left arm to opposite gent and dance back to place, passing right shoulder to right. (8 bars)

(e) Both couples swing. (8 bars)

(f) Top gent and opposite lady swing in the centre, reversing to place during the last two bars. During this time, their partners turn slowly anticlockwise in place. (8 bars)

(g) Both couples square again, as in (b). (8 bars)

(h) Top lady and opposite gent swing in the centre, reversing to place during the last two bars. Again, their partners turn slowly in place.

(8 bars)

(i) Both couples square again. (8 bars)

(j) Ladies chain – right hands in the centre, left arm around the opposite gent, turning to finish on his left-hand side, facing in, to form a circle of four in the centre for the basket. (8 bars)

(k) Both couples swing in a circle of four in the centre (6 bars) and reverse to place. (8 bars)

(l) Both couples advance and retire twice, holding hands in front. (8 bars)

(m) Both couples swing to finish. (8 bars)

FIGURE 2: POLKA (168 BARS)

(a) Both couples house around in waltz hold. (8 bars)

(b) Both couples dance the 'walkabout'. They dance an anticlockwise square around the set. Gents begin by stepping (1 2, 1 2 3) to the lady's position on their right, then dance on the spot there, turning slightly anticlockwise while the ladies begin by crossing (1 2, 1 2 3) to the opposite gent's position and then dance on the spot there, turning slightly anticlockwise. All continue to each successive position until they are back at home. (16 bars)

(c) Both couples swing in waltz hold. (8 bars)

(d) Both couples now dance 'sevens' across the set, gents passing back to back. They dance fourteen steps on the way over. Changing weight to the other foot, they dance sevens back to place, ladies passing back to back this time. (8 bars)

(e) Both couples house around each other. (8 bars)

(f) Repeat (d) and (e). (16 bars)

(g) Top ladies chain, as in Figure 1 (d). (8 bars)

(h) Both couples swing in place. (8 bars)

(i) Gents advance to the centre (1 2, 1 2 3), left shoulder to left, and dance on the spot (1 2 3, 1 2 3), turning slightly to face each other, then continue to the opposite gent's position and dance anticlockwise into place there. (8 bars)

(j) All swing new partners. (8 bars)

(k) Facing their new partners, both couples slide to the centre and back, then slide in again, passing through the other couple, and pass their partners left shoulder to left as they dance into opposite positions. Ladies turn anticlockwise and gents turn clockwise into place. (8 bars)

(l) All repeat (k), returning to home positions. (8 bars)

(m) All swing new partners. (8 bars)

(n) Gents repeat (i), crossing back to their own places. (8 bars)

(o) All swing their own partners again. (8 bars)

(p) Both couples dance the Walkabout, as in (b). (16 bars)

(q) Both couples dance around the house. (8 bars)

FIGURE 3: REEL (144 BARS)

(a) Holding crossed hands, both couples lead around, gents turning the lady clockwise under the left hand during the last two bars. (8 bars)

(b) Hooking left arm in left with their partners, all dance around in place, turning anticlockwise twice to face their partners during the last two bars. (8 bars)

(c) Both couples swing in *céilí* hold. (8 bars)

(d) Both gents place their right arm over their partner's shoulder, taking their partner's right hand in their right and left hand in their left. While the second couple stay in place, the first couple advance and retire, then advance again, and the leading lady turns clockwise to stand beside the second gent, taking his left hand in her left. The top gent now takes the ladies' free hands as he stands facing the line of three. (8 bars)

(e) All dance across the set and back (4 bars), then dance to the centre, and as both gents retire to their own places, ladies cross left shoulder to left to opposite positions (4 bars). (8 bars)

(f) All swing new partners. (8 bars)

(g) Gents advance to take left arms in the centre and dance around each other twice, then double the last two bars to meet their own partners in opposite positions, taking crossed hands. (8 bars)

(h) Repeat (a) to (g) with second couple leading. This time the gents will meet their own partners at home at (g). (56 bars)

(i) Repeat (a) to (c) to finish. (24 bars)

FIGURE 4: FLING

(a) Taking waltz hold, all couples face slightly anticlockwise around the room in a big circle, with gents almost facing the wall and ladies almost facing towards the centre. Gents begin with their weight on their right leg and ladies begin with their weight on their left leg. All hop on this foot, then step down on the other one (gent's left and lady's right), with the gents stepping forward (towards the wall) and the ladies stepping backward (towards the wall), then hop on this foot and step back onto the first one, gents stepping backward and ladies stepping forward, and step sideways, gents to their left and ladies to their right (hop 1 2 3). They now repeat all the steps and movements with the ladies going backward on their left foot and the gents going forward on their right and then step sideways in the other direction (hop 1 2 3). This sequence is repeated from the beginning. (8 bars)

(b) All couples house, turning clockwise three times while moving anticlockwise around the room (6 bars), then double (2 bars) to finish with gents facing the wall again and ladies facing towards the centre. (8 bars)

(c) They repeat (a) and (b) a number of times, until either the dancers or the musicians decide to finish.

KILGARVAN POLKA SET

This Kerry set was recorded by Paddy Hanafin, dancing teacher and organiser of the Tralee Shindig.

FIGURE 1: POLKA (192 BARS)

(a) All couples take waltz hold and dance the body. Ladies reverse as gents dance forward to the next position and turn once they are there. The movements are repeated three times as they dance around the set. (16 bars)

(b) All couples dance around the house. (8 bars)

(c) Top couples dance the star with the side couple on their left. They join right hands and dance around, then join left hands and dance back to place. (8 bars)

(d) All couples swing in waltz hold. (8 bars)

(e) Repeat (a) to (d), dancing (c) with the couple on the other side. (40 bars)

(f) All dance (a) to (e) again. (80 bars)

(g) All dance the body and house again. (24 bars)

FIGURE 2: POLKA (112 BARS)

(a) All dance the body and house, as in Figure 1. (24 bars)

(b) Top couples house around each other. (8 bars)

(c) Top couples square to opposite side and house back to place. (8 bars)

(d) All dance the body and house again. (24 bars)

(e) Side couples dance (b) and (c). (16 bars)

(f) All dance the body and house again. (24 bars)

FIGURE 3: POLKA (112 BARS)

(a) All dance the body and house, as in Figure 1. (24 bars)

(b) The four ladies join right hands in the centre, chain with left hand around the opposite gent, give right hands in the centre again and dance to home. (8 bars)

(c) All couples swing in place. (8 bars)

(d) All dance the body and house again. (24 bars)

(e) Repeat (b) and (c). (16 bars)

(f) All dance the body and house. (24 bars)

FIGURE 4: JIG (112 BARS)

(a) All dance the body and house, as in Figure 1. (24 bars)

(b) Top couples slide to the centre and back in waltz hold, then top ladies cross right shoulder to right and top gents cross left shoulder to left. (8 bars)

(c) Top couples repeat (b), crossing back to home. (8 bars)

(c) All dance the body and house. (24 bars)

(d) Side couples dance (b) and (c). (16 bars)

(e) All dance the body and house. (24 bars)

FIGURE 5: SLIDE (144 BARS)

(a) All dance the body and house, as in Figure 1. (24 bars)

(b) Top couples house around each other. (8 bars)

(c) Top couples slide to the centre, then house to the opposite side. (8 bars)

(d) Top ladies chain with right hands in the centre, with left hands as they turn around the opposite gent, with right hands in the centre again and then dance back to place. (8 bars)

(e) Top couples slide to the centre and house across to home. (8 bars)

(f) All dance the body and house. (24 bars)

(g) Side couples dance (b) to (e). (32 bars)

(h) All dance the body and house, as in Figure 1. (24 bars)

FIGURE 6: HORNPIPE (160 BARS)

(a) All dance the body and house, as in Figure 1. In the body, they dance as follows: hop, in 2 3, stamp, back 2 3, then turn to the position on the right and repeat the movements three times, dancing around the set to home. (24 bars)

(b) To change partners, all advance and retire three times in a circle, dancing in (hop 1 2 3) and back (stamp 1 2 3), then the gents dance in on their own as the ladies move outside them to the next lady's position on the right. (8 bars)

(c) Repeat (a) and (b) three times, the ladies dancing with each gent in turn to get back to their own partners. (96 bars)

(d) All dance the body and house again to finish. (24 bars)

KILLYON SET

This set, as remembered by Jack Grogan, was recorded in 1998 by Nora Carroll of Kilcormac, County Offaly. Jack remembered the set being danced at house dances in the 1920s and 1930s.

FIGURE 1 : POLKA (168 BARS)

(a) Top couples pass through to the other side, ladies passing between the opposite couple; all turn clockwise, pass back to their own side and face their partners. (8 bars)

(b) Swing in place in *céilí* hold. (8 bars)

(c) Ladies chain with right hands in the centre, turn with left hand under the opposite gent's left arm and dance back to turn under their partner's right hand into place with the gent's arm over the lady's shoulder. (8 bars)

(d) Lead around, with the gent's right arm over the lady's shoulder, holding both hands. (8 bars)

(e) Top couples swing in *céilí* hold. (8 bars)

(f) Side couples dance (a) to (e). (40 bars)

(g) Repeat (a) to (f), with top couples and side couples dancing again. (80 bars)

FIGURE 2 : POLKA (72 BARS)

(a) All couples advance and retire holding both hands. Each gent brings his right arm back over the lady's head as they retire, to rest his arm on her shoulder (4 bars). All now lead anticlockwise to opposite positions, each gent bringing his right hand forward over the lady's head as they reach the other side (4 bars). (8 bars)

(b) All couples swing in opposite positions. (8 bars)

(c) Repeat (a), dancing back to place. (8 bars)

(d) All couples swing in place. (8 bars)

(d) Dance (a) to (d) again. (32 bars)

FIGURE 3 : JIG (136 BARS)

(a) Top couples pass through (2 bars), turn in towards their partners until facing back, lady anticlockwise and gent clockwise (2 bars) and take left arm in left with the opposite lady or gent. They now pass through to their own side, holding this person's left hand and, taking their own partner's right hand in right over the lady's shoulder, lead to opposite position where the lady turns anticlockwise under her partner's right hand (4 bars). (8 bars)

(b) Both couples swing in the opposite position in *céilí* hold. (8 bars)

(c) With all starting by stepping onto their inside foot, both couples dance 'sevens' to the centre and back and house back to their own places, dancing in *céilí* hold all the time. (8 bars)

(d) Both couples swing in place. (8 bars)

(e) Side couples dance (a) to (d). (32 bars)

(f) Repeat (a) to (e), top couples and side couples dancing again. (64 bars)

FIGURE 4 : REEL (176 BARS)

(a) Ladies chain, turning under the opposite gent's arm and dancing back to turn under their own partner's arm, as in the Plain Set.

(8 bars)

(b) Both couples swing in *céilí* hold. (8 bars)

(c) While second top couple stand in place in *céilí* hold, first top couple gallop across and back (4 bars), then turn one and a half times to finish in front of the other couple, facing back towards their own places. The two ladies are on the same side and the gents are on the same side, with one couple in front of the other as they face towards the first top position. (8 bars)

(d) Both couples, moving in the same direction, now dance 'sevens' towards first top position and back, then turn clockwise twice, to finish with each couple in the position opposite their own.

(8 bars)

(e) Both couples dance 'sevens' into the centre and back, then house across to their own positions. (8 bars)

(f) Side couples dance (a) to (e), with the first side couple (on the left) leading. (40 bars)

(g) Repeat (a) to (f), with top couples and side couples dancing again. This time, the second top couple and second side couple lead.

(80 bars)

(h) All couples swing. (8 bars)

FIGURE 5 : JIG OR POLKA (136 BARS)

(a) All couples house around twice. (16 bars)

(b) Circle, advance and retire twice. (8 bars)

(c) All swing in place. (8 bars)

(d) Ladies move on the outside to the right and lead around with the next gent. Each gent's arm is around the lady's waist. (8 bars)

(e) Repeat (b) to (d) until ladies are back leading around with their own partners again. (72 bars)

(f) Circle, advance and retire twice. (8 bars)

(g) All swing with their own partners to finish. (8 bars)

KNOCKNABOUL SET

This set, from County Limerick, was given to me by Eileen O'Doherty, dancing teacher and author of The Walking Polka.

FIGURE 1: SLIDE (104 BARS)

(a) Top couples, in waltz hold, slide to the centre, slide back and turn once in place. (8 bars)

(b) Top ladies chain. They take right hands in the centre, turn twice with left arm around opposite gent, pass right shoulder to right in the centre again and dance back to place. (8 bars)

(c) Top couples swing in waltz hold. (8 bars)

(d) Side couples dance (a) to (c). (24 bars)

(e) Top couples repeat (a) to (c). (24 bars)

(f) Side couples repeat (a) to (c). (24 bars)

FIGURE 2: SLIDE (136 BARS)

(a) Top couples, in waltz hold, slide to the centre, slide back and turn once in place. (8 bars)

(b) Top ladies cross and swing with opposite gents. (8 bars)

(c) With new partners, top couples slide to the centre, slide back and turn once in place. (8 bars)

(d) Top ladies cross back and swing with their own partners. (8 bars)

(e) Side couples dance (a) to (d). (32 bars)

(f) Top couples repeat (a) to (d). (32 bars)

(g) Side couples repeat (a) to (d). (32 bars)

FIGURE 3: SLIDE (168 BARS)

(a) Top couples, in waltz hold, slide to the centre, slide back and turn once in place. (8 bars)

(b) Top gent and opposite lady swing in the centre (6 bars), reversing to place during the last two bars. (8 bars)

(c) Top couples, in waltz hold, slide to the centre, slide back and turn once in place. (8 bars)

(d) Top lady and opposite gent swing in the centre (6 bars), reversing to place during the last two bars. (8 bars)

(e) Top couples, in waltz hold, slide to the centre, slide back and turn once in place. (8 bars)

(f) Side couples dance (a) to (e). First side couple are on the left. (40 bars)

(f) Top couples repeat (a) to (e).   (40 bars)

(g) Side couples repeat (a) to (e).   (40 bars)

FIGURE 4: POLKA OR FAST REEL (104 BARS)

(a) In waltz hold, gents reverse their partners anticlockwise all round
the house.   (8 bars)

(b) All couples house around.   (8 bars)

(c) Top couples slide to the centre and back, then house to opposite
positions.   (8 bars)

(d) Top couples slide to the centre and back, then house to home
positions.   (8 bars)

(e) All four ladies give right hands in the centre, turn with left arm
around opposite gent, give right hands in the centre again and
dance back to home.   (8 bars)

(f) All couples swing in place.   (8 bars)

(g) Repeat (a) to (f) with side couples dancing (c) and (d).   (48 bars)

FIGURE 5: HORNPIPE (160 BARS)

(a) All couples dance one step to the centre and back, then turn
clockwise to the position on the right (4 bars). Repeat the
movements three times, dancing around to home (12 bars).

                                                                      (16 bars)

(b) All couples dance around the house.   (8 bars)

(c) The four gents stand in place as the ladies move on to the position
on the right.   (8 bars)

(d) All repeat (a) to (c) three times as the ladies move around the set,
dancing with each gent in turn before returning to their partners.

                                                                      (96 bars)

(e) All dance (a) and (b) with their own partners to finish.   (24 bars)

Knocktopher Polka Set

This set was given to me by Brigid Collins of Stripp, Furbo, County Galway; Brigid is originally from County Kilkenny. The step danced in the advance and retire jig figure is the céilí 'sink and grind' step – tap down, up (kicking the same foot forward), 1 2 3.

Figure 1: Polka (104 bars)

(a) Taking their partner's right hand in their right, all couples chain all round, ladies clockwise and gents anticlockwise. (16 bars)

(b) All couples swing in place. (8 bars)

(c) Top couples house around each other twice. (16 bars)

(d) Side couples house around each other twice. (16 bars)

(e) Top couples house around each other twice. (16 bars)

(f) Side couples house around each other twice. (16 bars)

(g) All couples swing in place to finish. (8 bars)

Figure 2: Polka (88 bars)

(a) All couples lead around anticlockwise, each gent with his arm around the lady's waist and her arm on his shoulder. (8 bars)

(b) Top couples house around each other. (8 bars)

(c) Top couples advance and retire, then house to opposite positions. (8 bars)

(d) Top couples advance and retire, then house across to their own positions. (8 bars)

(e) Top couples house around each other again. (8 bars)

(f) Side couples house around each other. (8 bars)

(g) Side couples advance and retire, then house to opposite positions. (8 bars)

(h) Side couples advance and retire, then house across to their own positions. (8 bars)

(i) Side couples house around each other again. (8 bars)

(j) All couples house around to finish. (8 bars)

Figure 3: Polka (72 bars)

(a) Top couples house around each other. (8 bars)

(b) All couples lead around anticlockwise, each gent with his arm around the lady's waist and her arm on his shoulder. (8 bars)

(c) Top couples house around each other. (8 bars)

(d) All couples lead around anticlockwise, each gent with his arm around the lady's waist and her arm on his shoulder. (8 bars)

(e) Top couples house around each other. (8 bars)

(f) All couples lead around anticlockwise, each gent with his arm around the lady's waist and her arm on his shoulder. (8 bars)

(g) Top couples house around each other. (8 bars)

(h) All couples lead around anticlockwise, each gent with his arm around the lady's waist and her arm on his shoulder. (8 bars)

FIGURE 4: JIG (104 BARS)

(a) All advance and retire twice in a circle. (8 bars)

(b) All couples swing in place. (8 bars)

(c) As the gents turn slightly clockwise to meet them, all the ladies move up on the outside to join the next gent on their right and lead around with him. (8 bars)

(d) Repeat (a) to (c) three times, so that all finish leading around with their own partners. (72 bars)

LONG CALEDONIAN SET

(NORTH CLARE)

Notes on this version of the Clare Caledonian Set were first given to me by Aidan Vaughan of Milltown Malbay. Aidan got the set from Dick Grant of Lahinch.

FIGURE 1: REEL (72 BARS)
(a) All advance and retire twice in a circle.   (8 bars)
(b) All couples swing in waltz hold.   (8 bars)
(c) All couples advance and retire in waltz hold (4 bars), then dance around to opposite positions (4 bars).   (8 bars)
(d) All couples advance, retire and dance around to home.   (8 bars)
(e) All couples house around.   (8 bars)
(f) All repeat (c) to (e).   (24 bars)

FIGURE 2: REEL (48 BARS)
(a) All advance and retire twice in a circle.   (8 bars)
(b) All couples swing in place.   (8 bars)
(c) All couples house around.   (8 bars)
(d) All couples dance at home.   (8 bars)
(e) All couples house around again.   (8 bars)

FIGURE 3: REEL (88 BARS)
(a) All advance and retire twice in a circle.   (8 bars)
(b) All couples swing in place.   (8 bars)
(c) All couples advance and retire, then dance around to opposite positions.   (8 bars)
(d) All couples advance and retire again, then dance around to home. (8 bars)
(e) All couples advance and retire, then dance around to opposite positions again.   (8 bars)
(f) All couples house around.   (8 bars)
(g) Starting in opposite positions, all couples repeat (c) to (f), to finish at home.   (32 bars)

FIGURE 4: JIG (152 BARS)
(a) All advance and retire twice in a circle.   (8 bars)
(b) All couples swing.   (8 bars)

(c) All couples advance and retire (4 bars), then, passing inside their own partners, gents dance on to the lady on their right. (8 bars)

(d) All house with new partners. (8 bars)

(e) All repeat (c) and (d), gents moving on to each lady on their right and arriving back to their own partners for the last house. (48 bars)

(f) All repeat (c) to (e). (64 bars)

FIGURE 5: REEL (104 BARS)

(a) All advance and retire twice in a circle. (8 bars)

(b) All couples swing in place. (8 bars)

(c) All couples advance and retire, then dance around to opposite positions. (8 bars)

(d) All couples advance and retire, then dance around to home. (8 bars)

(e) All repeat (b) and (c). (16 bars)

(f) All couples house around. (8 bars)

(g) All repeat (c) to (f). (40 bars)

FIGURE 6: HORNPIPE (176 BARS)

(a) All advance and retire twice in a circle. (8 bars)

(b) All couples swing in place. (8 bars)

(c) In waltz hold, all couples dance in and back (2 bars), then turn clockwise once, moving to the position on the right (2 bars). Repeat the movements three times, dancing on to each position until back at home. (16 bars)

(d) All couples house around. (8 bars)

(e) All couples advance and retire, then ladies move on to the gent on their right. (8 bars)

(f) All dance (c), (d) and (e) three times, ladies dancing on to new partners until back with their own partners again. (96 bars)

(g) All dance (c) and (d) with their own partners to finish. (24 bars)

Loughgraney Half Set

This half-set was given to me by Ciarán Condron of Dublin. Ciarán learned the set from Michael and Mary Sheedy. The 'down' or 'polka' step is danced for the jig figure.

Figure 1: Reel (88 bars)

(a) Forming a circle of four, the dancers advance and retire twice.   (8 bars)

(b) Both couples dance at home in waltz hold.   (8 bars)

(c) The two couples dance a full house around each other.   (8 bars)

(d) Both couples dance across to the opposite side, each lady passing between the opposite couple. At the opposite side, partners pass each other left shoulder to left and face back. They dance the same movements back again to place.   (8 bars)

(e) The two couples dance a full house around each other.   (8 bars)

(f) Repeat (b) to (e).   (32 bars)

(g) Both couple swing in place in waltz hold. Locally this is called the full wheel.   (8 bars)

Figure 2: Reel (104 bars)

(a) Forming a circle of four, the dancers advance and retire twice.   (8 bars)

(b) Both couples dance at home in waltz hold.   (8 bars)

(c) The two couples dance a full house around each other.   (8 bars)

(d) The two couples advance and retire once in waltz hold, then pass through to opposite positions and pass left shoulder to left into place there.   (8 bars)

(e) The two couples advance and retire once in waltz hold, then pass back to their own positions and pass left shoulder to left into place there.   (8 bars)

(f) The two couples dance a full house around each other.   (8 bars)

(g) Repeat (b) to (f).   (40 bars)

(h) Both couple swing in place in waltz hold.   (8 bars)

Figure 3: Reel (136 bars)

(a) Forming a circle of four, the dancers advance and retire twice.   (8 bars)

(b) Both couples dance at home in waltz hold.   (8 bars)

(c) The two couples dance a full house around each other.   (8 bars)

(d) In waltz hold, both couples advance and retire, then house across to opposite positions.   (8 bars)

(e) Both couples advance and retire again and dance back to home
   positions. (8 bars)
(f) The two couples dance a full house around each other. (8 bars)
(g) Both couples dance at home in waltz hold. (8 bars)
(h) The two couples dance a full house around each other. (8 bars)
(i) Repeat (b) to (h). (56 bars)
(j) Both couples swing in place in waltz hold. (8 bars)

FIGURE 4: JIG (152 BARS)

(a) Forming a circle of four, the dancers advance and retire twice. (8 bars)
(b) Both couples dance at home in waltz hold. (8 bars)
(c) The two couples dance a full house around each other. (8 bars)
(d) Ladies chain with right hands in the centre, turn under the
   opposite gent's left arm while dancing around him, pass back to
   place and turn anticlockwise under their own partner's right hand.
   (8 bars)
(e) Both couples dance at home in waltz hold. (8 bars)
(f) First couple dance across and leave the lady beside the second
   gent, who takes each lady's outside hand. The first gent does not
   hold the ladies' hands. (8 bars)
(g) As the first gent retires to place, the line of three advances and
   retires once, then advances across the set. The ladies turn in, first
   lady clockwise and second lady anticlockwise, turning under the
   second gent's arms to stand beside the first gent. The first gent
   now holds the ladies' outside hands and the second gent stands
   alone. (8 bars)
(h) The ladies repeat (g) with the first gent, turning in to form a circle
   of four. (8 bars)
(i) The two couples swing in four in the centre. (8 bars)
(j) Ladies chain again. (8 bars)
(k) Both couples dance at home in waltz hold. (8 bars)
(l) Repeat (f) to (k) with second couple leading. (48 bars)
(m) Both couples swing in place in waltz hold. (8 bars)

FIGURE 5: REEL: (136 BARS)

(a) Forming a circle of four, the dancers advance and retire twice. (8 bars)
(b) Both couples dance at home in waltz hold. (8 bars)
(c) The two couples dance a full house around each other. (8 bars)
(d) Both couples advance and retire once in waltz hold, then the two
   ladies change places, passing right shoulder to right and turning

115

one and a half times to face the opposite gent. While the ladies are crossing, the gents turn clockwise in place. (8 bars)

(e) The two couples dance a full house around each other. (8 bars)

(f) Both couples dance at home in waltz hold. (8 bars)

(g) Both couples advance and retire once in waltz hold, then the two ladies change places, passing right shoulder to right and turning one and a half times to face their own partners. While the ladies are crossing, the gents turn clockwise in place. (8 bars)

(h) The two couples dance a full house around each other. (8 bars)

(i) Repeat (b) to (h). (56 bars)

(j) Both couple swing in place in waltz hold. (8 bars)

FIGURE 6: HORNPIPE (176 BARS)

(a) Forming a circle of four, the dancers advance and retire twice. (8 bars)

(b) Both couples dance at home in waltz hold. (8 bars)

(c) In waltz hold, both couples dance the body. They dance one step to the centre and back, turn clockwise to the next position on the right (4 bars), then repeat those movements three times, dancing around the set. (16 bars)

(d) Both couples dance around the house in waltz hold. (8 bars)

(e) Both couples advance and retire once in waltz hold, then ladies move to the side position on their right while the gents move to the side position on their left, all turning clockwise one and a half times. (8 bars)

(f) In waltz hold, both couples dance the body. They dance one step to the centre and back, turn clockwise to the next position on the right (4 bars), then repeat those movements three times, dancing around the set. (16 bars)

(g) Both couples dance around the house in waltz hold. (8 bars)

(h) All advance and retire, then change partners again, thus meeting their own partners in opposite top positions. (8 bars)

(i) Repeat (c) to (h), all meeting opposite partners in the other side position, then their own partners again back at home. (64 bars)

(j) All dance the body and house again with their own partners. (24 bars)

LOUGH NEAGH SET

This set was first described to me by Pete Brett from Philadelphia, who visited the Joe Mooney Summer School in Drumshanbo. It had been danced for many years by Irish–American dancers; Pete sent me their notes on the set, as written by Jean Ver Hoeven. A few years later, Pete and I met again, and he put me in touch with Jean, who kindly provided a video recording of the set; these notes are based on that recording. In the set, the first side couple are on the right-hand side of the first top couple.

FIGURE 1: REELS (152 BARS)

(a) Taking their partner's right hand in their right, top couples face the side couple on their left and side couples face the top couple on their right. All advance and retire once (4 bars), then pass through the other couple and move forward to meet the next couple coming towards them (4 bars). When passing through, ladies pass between the opposite couple and gents pass on the outside.   (8 bars)

(b) Repeat (a) three times, top couples moving clockwise around the set while side couples move anticlockwise around it.   (24 bars)

(c) Top ladies move to the centre touching right hands, then give their left hand to the side gent on their left, taking the side gent's right hand. The side gent holds his partner's right hand in his left. The top lady dances under an arch made by the side couple and then dances in an anticlockwise circle all round the side couple, while the side lady dances under the arch twice, followed by the gent. Finally the top lady comes out under the arch to meet her partner and all couples swing in waltz hold.   (16 bars)

(d) Side ladies move to the centre touching right hands, then give their left hand to the top gent on their left, taking the top gent's right hand. The top gent holds his partner's right hand in his left. The side lady dances under an arch made by the top couple, then dances in an anticlockwise circle all round the top couple, while the top lady dances under the arch twice, followed by the gent. Finally the side lady comes out under the arch.   (8 bars)

(e) All dance to meet their partners and swing in waltz hold.   (8 bars)

(f) Top couples face the side couple on their left and pass through, with the side couple in the centre holding inside hands. All take the opposite person's free hand as they pass through, turn around them and face back. Top couples now pass back through the centre, holding their partner's inside hand, and all move forward to face the couple on the other side. (8 bars)

(g) All repeat (f) with the couple on the other side. This time, the top couples cross through the centre and pass back on the outside. (8 bars)

(h) Top gents chain with right hands in the centre and dance into the opposite gent's position, facing the opposite lady. They now dance back to back with the lady, passing forward left shoulder to left and reversing back right shoulder to right. (8 bars)

(i) Top gents chain with left hands in the centre and dance into their own positions, facing their partners. They now dance back to back with her, passing forward right shoulder to right and reversing back left shoulder to left. (8 bars)

(j) Side couples dance (h) and (i). (16 bars)

(k) All repeat (a) and (b). (32 bars)

FIGURE 2: REEL (144 BARS)

(a) Taking their partner's right hand in their right, top couples face the side couple on their left and side couples face the top couple on their right. All advance and retire once (4 bars), then pass through the other couple and move forward to meet the next couple coming towards them (4 bars). When passing through, ladies pass between the opposite couple and gents pass on the outside. (8 bars)

(b) Repeat (a) three times, top couples moving clockwise around the set while side couples move anticlockwise. (24 bars)

(c) Top couples house around each other inside. (8 bars)

(d) Top couples face the couple on their right and dance a square chain. All dance forward, taking the opposite person's right hand as they pass, then they take their own partner's left hand as they pass on the second side of the square (4 bars). They continue, taking the opposite person's right hand again and, finally, their own partner's left hand as they dance back to place. (8 bars)

(e) Side couples house inside. (8 bars)

(f) All dance the square chain again, side couples going to their right this time. (8 bars)

(g) All couples dance at home. (32 bars)

(h) All couples house inside in turn – first top couple, first side couple (on the right), second top couple and second side couple. (8 bars)

(i) All repeat (a) and (b). (32 bars)

FIGURE 3: HORNPIPE (104 BARS)

(a) All couples face into the set, with the gent's right arm around the lady's waist, holding right hand in right and left hand in left. They advance and retire once, then ladies move on to the right, passing outside the next gent and stepping into place beside him.　　(8 bars)

(b) Repeat (a) three times, ladies dancing with each gent as they move around the set.　　(24 bars)

(c) The four gents weave or interlace slowly to their right, passing inside their own partners, outside the next lady and inside the third lady, and dance into place, facing their own partners.　　(16 bars)

(d) All couples house around.　　(8 bars)

(e) Top couples face the side couple on their right. All couples dance around the couple facing them, housing across (hop 1 2 3, hop 1 2 3) and doubling back to their own places (hop 1, hop 2, hop 3, hop 4).　　(4 bars)

(f) All repeat (e), dancing around the couple on the other side.　　(4 bars)

(g) All face their own partners, take right hand in right and chain all round. After passing their own partners, the gents take the next lady's left hand in their left and the lady turns clockwise under his arm as they pass by. They now take the third lady's right hand in their right as they pass, and, taking left hand in left, the fourth lady turns clockwise under the gent's arm again as they pass through opposite positions (8 bars). They continue around until back at home.　　(16 bars)

(h) Taking waltz hold, all couples dance the body. They step in, step back, then turn to the next position on the right (4 bars) and repeat the movements three times, dancing all round the set.　　(16 bars)

FIGURE 4: REELS (160 BARS)

(a) Taking their partner's right hand in right, top couples face the side couple on their left and side couples face the top couple on their right. All advance and retire once (4 bars), then pass through the other couple and move forward to meet the next couple coming towards them (4 bars). When passing through, ladies pass between the opposite couple and gents pass on the outside.　　(8 bars)

(b) Repeat (a) three times, top couples moving clockwise around the set while side couples move anticlockwise.　　(24 bars)

(c) The four ladies advance to the centre, turn anticlockwise to face their own partners and dance back to back with them, passing forward right shoulder to right and reversing back left shoulder to left. Ladies finish facing out from the gents' positions, with the gents facing in from the ladies' positions. (8 bars)

(d) The four gents advance to the centre, turn anticlockwise to face their own partners and dance back to back with them, all passing forward right shoulder to right and reversing back left shoulder to left into their own positions. (8 bars)

(e) All couples swing in waltz hold. (8 bars)

(f) Taking their partner's right hand, all chain halfway, gents going anticlockwise and ladies clockwise. All turn around their partners at the opposite side to face back the way they came (8 bars). They now chain back, gents going clockwise this time (8 bars). (16 bars)

(g) Passing straight through their own positions from (f), all continue the chain to opposite positions again, turn around their partners, chain back (12 bars) and swing in place (4 bars). (16 bars)

(h) As they face anticlockwise around the set, each gent now turns the lady clockwise to his left-hand side under the hand held while swinging (gent's left, lady's right), then, taking right hand in right, they lead forward one position to the right (4 bars). While the gents dance on the spot, the ladies move on, passing inside the next gent on the right and taking his right hand in her right to turn anticlockwise in front of him under his arm into place outside him (4 bars). (8 bars)

(i) All swing their new partners. (8 bars)

(j) Repeat (h) and (i) three times. Ladies move around the set twice as they dance with each gent, while the gents dance around the set once as they dance with each lady in turn. All finish by swinging their own partners. (48 bars)

MAYO LANCERS SET

This set was taught by Martin Bolger at the Galway International Set Dancing Festival in 1998. Thanks to Mickey Kelly for additional help and information with the set, especially Figure 7.

FIGURE 1 (HOUSE): JIG (72 BARS)

(a) All dance anticlockwise around the set in single file, each gent behind his partner. During the last two bars, all take right hand in right and ladies turn clockwise under the gent's right arm to face him. (8 bars)

(b) All couples swing in the old *céilí* hold, right hand in right (palms), each of them holding their partner's elbow. (8 bars)

(c) Top ladies double-chain – take right arm in right and turn clockwise twice around each other in the centre, then take their partner's left arm in left and turn anticlockwise around him into place. (8 bars)

(d) Top couples house in waltz hold. (8 bars)

(e) All couples swing. (8 bars)

(f) Side couples dance (c) and (d) and all swing again. (24 bars)

FIGURE 2 (SQUARE): JIG (152 BARS)

(a) All dance anticlockwise around the set in single file, each gent behind his partner. During the last two bars, all take right hand in right and ladies turn clockwise under the gent's right arm to face him. (8 bars)

(b) All couples swing in the old *céilí* hold. (8 bars)

(c) Top ladies double-chain, as in Figure 1(c). (8 bars)

(d) Top couples square. They cross the set, ladies passing between the opposite couple and gents on the outside, then partners pass left shoulder to left through the opposite position and repeat the movements back to place, to finish facing the corners. (8 bars)

(e) All swing the person facing them in the corner. (8 bars)

(f) All swing their own partners. (8 bars)

(g) Side couples dance (c) and (d), then all dance (e) and (f). (32 bars)

(h) Repeat (c) to (g), top couples and side couples leading again. (64 bars)

FIGURE 3 (LINES): REEL (120 BARS)

(a) All dance anticlockwise around the set in single file, each gent behind his partner. During the last two bars, all take right hand in right and ladies turn clockwise under the gent's right arm to face him. (8 bars)

(b) All couples swing in the old *céilí* hold. (8 bars)

(c) Top ladies double-chain, as in Figure 1(c), with top couples turning into place, left arm in left and backing away from their partners to line up in side positions. (8 bars)

(d) All advance and retire in lines of four and advance again. Side couples retire while top couples dance out facing their partners. (8 bars)

(e) All swing their own partners. (8 bars)

(f) Side couples repeat (c) and all repeat (d) and (e). (24 bars)

(g) Repeat (c) to (f), top couples and side couples leading again. (48 bars)

FIGURE 4 (PÓIGÍN): POLKA (120 BARS)

(a) All dance anticlockwise around the set in single file, each gent behind his partner. During the last two bars, all take right hand in right and ladies turn clockwise under the gent's right arm to face him. (8 bars)

(b) All couples swing in the old *céilí* hold. (8 bars)

(c) Top ladies double-chain, as in Figure 1(c). (8 bars)

(d) Keeping their hands behind their backs, top dancers advance and retire singly, then advance, kiss the opposite person and retire.

(8 bars)

(e) All couples swing in place. (8 bars)

(f) Side couples dance (c) and (d). (16 bars)

(g) All couples swing. (8 bars)

(h) Repeat (c) to (g). (48 bars)

FIGURE 5 (FLING): FLING (88 BARS)

(a) All couples dance in place, turning twice in waltz hold. (8 bars)

(b) Top gents take their partner's left hand in their right and the nearest side lady's right hand in their left. All dance toe (to the side), heel, toe on their right foot, then dance (1 2 3), stepping to the right. They now dance toe, heel, toe on their left foot and dance (1 2 3), stepping to the left. Side gents dance alone. (4 bars)

(c) All repeat (b), dancing to the right and to the left again. (4 bars)

(d) Each side lady dances clockwise under an arch made by the top couple, followed by the top gent, while her own partner dances one turn in place. (4 bars)

(e) All ladies turn clockwise once under their partner's arm, right hand in right. (4 bars)

(f) Repeat (b) to (e) with side couples leading and top ladies joining them. (16 bars)

(g) All repeat (b) to (f) with top couples and side couples leading again. (32 bars)

(h) All couples dance around the house to finish. (8 bars)

FIGURE 6 ('BUNDLES OF FUN'): JIG (88 BARS)

(a) All dance anticlockwise around the set in single file, each gent behind his partner. During the last two bars, all take right hand in right and ladies turn clockwise under the gent's right arm to face him. (8 bars)

(b) All couples swing in the old *céilí* hold. (8 bars)

(c) Top couples house around the side couple on their right. (8 bars)

(d) Top ladies double-chain with the side lady on their right. (8 bars)

(e) Top couples swing in four with the side couple on their right. This swing is the 'bundle of fun'. All swing for six bars and reverse to place. (8 bars)

(f) Repeat (c) to (e), dancing with the couple on the other side. (24 bars)

(g) All couples house around. (8 bars)

(h) All swing in one circle, turning clockwise once. (8 bars)

FIGURE 7: POLKA (88 BARS)

(a) In waltz hold, all couples dance 'sevens' to the centre, two 'threes' there, 'sevens' back to place and 'threes' again. (8 bars)

(b) All couples swing in place. (8 bars)

(c) All couples dance 'sevens' to the position on their right, 'threes' there, turning clockwise slightly, then, starting on the other foot, they dance 'sevens' to the next position (opposite their own) and 'threes' there again. They repeat the movements dancing around the set to home. (16 bars)

(d) All couples swing in place. (8 bars)

(e) Repeat (a) to (d). (40 bars)

123

MEALAGH VALLEY JIG SET

This set is sometimes called the West Cork Plain Set. It has been taught extensively and popularised by Timmy McCarthy. I learned the set at a workshop organised in Dublin by the Brooks Academy dancers, at which Timmy taught the set.

FIGURE 1: SLIDE (72 BARS)

(a) Each top lady places her left hand on the gent's shoulder and he places his arm around her waist. Both couples advance and retire twice.   (8 bars)

(b) Top couples swing in waltz hold.   (8 bars)

(c) Top ladies chain with right hands in the centre, turn with left arm around opposite gent and chain in the centre again as they cross back to place.   (8 bars)

(d) Top couples swing in waltz hold.   (8 bars)

(e) Side couples repeat (a) to (d).   (32 bars)

FIGURE 2: SLIDES (56 BARS)

(a) All couples advance and retire twice, then house to opposite positions in waltz hold.   (8 bars)

(b) All couples advance and retire twice, then house back to home in waltz hold.   (8 bars)

(c) All couples swing in waltz hold.   (8 bars)

(d) All repeat (a) to (c).   (24 bars)

FIGURE 3: SLIDE (136 BARS)

(a) Top gent and opposite lady swing in the centre (6 bars), reversing to place during the last two bars.   (8 bars)

(b) Top couples take crossed hands and cross slowly anticlockwise to opposite positions, turning the lady once.   (8 bars)

(c) Top gent and opposite lady swing in the centre (6 bars), reversing to place during the last two bars.   (8 bars)

(d) Top couples take crossed hands and cross slowly anticlockwise to opposite positions, turning the lady once.   (8 bars)

(e) Top couples repeat (a) to (d), with second gent and lady swinging.(32 bars)

(f) Side couples dance (a) to (e). The first side couple are on the left of the first top couple.   (64 bars)

FIGURE 4: SLIDE (200 BARS)

(a) Top ladies chain with right hands in the centre, turn with left arm around the opposite gent and chain in the centre again as they cross back to place. (8 bars)

(b) Top couples swing in waltz hold. (8 bars)

(c) Top couples slide to the centre and back (4 bars) and turn once in place (2 bars), then the second lady crosses over, giving her left hand to the top gent's left as he takes his partner's right hand in his right, and both ladies turn in under his arms to stand beside him (2 bars). The second gent takes the ladies' free hands as he faces the line of three. (8 bars)

(d) The line of three advances as the other gent reverses (2 bars). All dance on the spot (2 bars), then dance back to the first top position again and dance on the spot (4 bars). The ladies turn to stand beside the second gent during the last bar. (8 bars)

(e) The new line of three retires to the second position as the top gent dances forward (2 bars). All dance on the spot (2 bars), then all dance to the centre (2 bars) and the top gent pulls the ladies towards him as they turn out to form a circle, all arms around the waist. (8 bars)

(f) Top couples swing in four in the centre. (8 bars)

(g) Top couples repeat (a) to (f), with the second couple leading. They break back to place during the last two bars at (f). (48 bars)

(h) Side couples repeat (a) to (g). (96 bars)

FIGURE 5: SLIDE (96 BARS)

(a) All couples lead around, the gents' arms around the ladies' waists. (8 bars)

(b) All couples advance and retire twice, then house to opposite positions in waltz hold. (8 bars)

(c) All couples advance and retire twice, then house back to home in waltz hold. (8 bars)

(d) The four ladies join right hands in the centre, turn with left arms around the opposite gent, join right hands in the centre again and dance home. (8 bars)

(e) All couples swing in place. (8 bars)

(f) All repeat (a) to (e). (40 bars)

(g) All couples lead around, the gents' arms around the ladies' waists. (8 bars)

FIGURE 6: POLKA (264 BARS)

(a) All couples lead around holding crossed hands. (8 bars)

(b) Taking waltz hold, all couples dance the body or polka, as in the Borlin Polka Set. They jump on both feet, kick one foot (gent's right, lady's left) towards the centre (1 bar) and dance on the spot (1 bar), then turn once to the next position on the right (2 bars). These movements are repeated three times as they dance around the set (12 bars). (16 bars)

(c) All couples dance around the house. (8 bars)

(d) The four ladies join right hands in the centre and dance around, then join left hands and dance back, moving on to the next lady's position on the right. (8 bars)

(e) The four gents join right hands in the centre and dance around, then join left hands and dance back to place. (8 bars)

(f) All swing their new partners. (8 bars)

(g) All repeat (a) to (f) three times, until back swinging their own partners again. (168 bars)

(h) All repeat (a) to (c) with their own partners. (32 bars)

MEATH HALF SET

This half-set was given to the Dunderry Set Dancers in 1994 by the late Nicky Smith of Martry. When revived, it was danced, for the first time in many years, in Horan's Pub. According to Nicky, the set was danced in houses and at crossroads around the area up to the early 1940s. This area would include Martry, Ardbrackan and the Commons, outside Navan. At the request of the Dunderry Set Dancers, the set is dedicated to Nicky's memory. My thanks to Carmel O'Callaghan, originally from Ardbrackan, for her help in obtaining the details of the set.

FIGURE 1: POLKA (72 BARS)

(a) Both couples house around each other.   (8 bars)

(b) Ladies chain.   (8 bars)

(c) All four join left hands in the centre and dance around, then turn, put right hands in and dance back to place.   (8 bars)

(d) Both couples swing.   (8 bars)

(e) Repeat (a) to (d).   (32 bars)

FIGURE 2: POLKA (88 BARS)

(a) Both couples house around each other.   (8 bars)

(b) Ladies chain.   (8 bars)

(c) First gent and second lady swing in the centre.   (8 bars)

(d) All four join left hands in the centre and dance around, then turn, put right hands in and dance back to place.   (8 bars)

(e) The two couples swing in four in the centre.   (8 bars)

(f) Repeat (b) to (e) with first lady and second gent swinging in the centre.   (32 bars)

(g) Both couples swing in place.   (8 bars)

FIGURE 3: POLKA (72 BARS)

(a) Both couples house around each other.   (8 bars)

(b) Taking right hands in right with their partners, both couples advance and retire once, then cross to opposite positions, with the second couple passing under an arch made by the first couple. As they dance into opposite positions, gents pass on the outside, with each lady turning anticlockwise under her partner's right arm.   (8 bars)

(c) Repeat (b), dancing back to home positions. This time, the second

127

couple make the arch and the first couple pass under it on the way
across. (8 bars)

(d) Both couples swing in place. (8 bars)

(e) Repeat (a) to (d). (32 bars)

FIGURE 4: POLKA (152 BARS)

(a) Both couples house around each other. (8 bars)

(b) Both couples advance and retire twice in waltz hold. (8 bars)

(c) Both couples swing in place. (8 bars)

(d) As the second couple stand in place holding right hands, the first
couple house inside, to leave the lady beside the opposite gent.
The first gent takes the ladies' other hands. (8 bars)

(e) The line of three advances across the set as the other gent retires,
then retires as he advances. They cross again, and during the last
two bars the ladies turn to stand beside the other gent, all still
holding hands. (8 bars)

(f) Repeat (e), this time the ladies turning to face in and form a circle
of four in the centre of the set. (8 bars)

(g) All swing in four in the centre. (8 bars)

(h) Ladies chain. (8 bars)

(i) Both couples swing in place. (8 bars)

(j) Repeat (a) to (i) with second couple leading at (d). (72 bars)

FIGURE 5: POLKA (88 BARS)

(a) Both couples house around each other. (8 bars)

(b) Both couples advance and retire once, then house to opposite
positions. (8 bars)

(c) Both couples advance and retire once, then house to home
positions. (8 bars)

(d) The ladies chain, taking right arms to turn twice around each other
in the centre and dancing to opposite positions. (8 bars)

(e) Ladies swing with opposite gents in the gent's position. (8 bars)

(f) Repeat (a) to (e), so that all finish swinging their own partners. (40 bars)

MEELIN VICTORIA JIG SET

*This set, from County Cork, was described to me
by Seamus Ó Méalóid.*

FIGURE 1: JIG (152 BARS)

(a) All couples dance around the house in waltz hold, ladies reversing
to each position and gents dancing forward. They turn slightly
anticlockwise in each position. This movement is called
'shunting'. (8 bars)

(b) All couples house around, turning clockwise four times. (8 bars)

(c) Both top couples dance at home, turning once in place. (8 bars)

(d) Both top couples face the side couple on their right, all couples
taking their partner's right hand in their right. They advance (1 2,
1 2 3) and retire (1 2, 1 2 3) twice. (8 bars)

(e) Top couples swing in place. (8 bars)

(f) Top couples house around each other. (8 bars)

(g) All gents swing the lady on their left, then swing their partners. (16 bars)

(h) Repeat (a) to (g), with side couples leading. (64 bars)

(i) All couples repeat (a) and (b). (16 bars)

FIGURE 2: JIG (152 BARS)

(a) All couples dance around the house using the shunting movement.
(8 bars)

(b) All couples house around. (8 bars)

(c) Both top couples dance at home, turning once in place. (8 bars)

(d) Both couples face to the centre. Ladies cross over, passing right
shoulder to right, and gents cross, passing left shoulder to left,
then all cross back the same way . (8 bars)

(e) Top couples swing in place. (8 bars)

(f) Top couples house around each other. (8 bars)

(g) All gents swing the lady on the left, then swing their partners. (16 bars)

(h) Repeat (a) to (g) with side couples leading. (64 bars)

(i) All couples repeat (a) and (b). (16 bars)

FIGURE 3: JIG (200 BARS)

(a) All couples dance around the house, using the 'shunting'
movement. (8 bars)

(b) All couples house around. (8 bars)

(c) Both top couples dance at home, turning once in place. (8 bars)

(d) Top couples advance and retire holding near hands (4 bars), then the top lady and the second top gent change places, passing right shoulder to right (4 bars). The two gents are now in the top position and the two ladies are in the second top position. (8 bars)

(e) Top gents and ladies advance and retire once (4 bars). Then, all moving together, the second top gent crosses back to his own place, the top lady crosses from the second gent's place to the second lady's place and the second top lady crosses diagonally to the top lady's original place (4 bars). (8 bars)

(f) Top gents each swing the opposite lady. (8 bars)

(g) Both couples advance and retire, then ladies cross back to their own places, right shoulder to right. (8 bars)

(h) Top couples swing their own partners. (8 bars)

(i) Top couples house around each other. (8 bars)

(j) All gents swing the lady on the left, then swing their partners. (16 bars)

(k) Repeat (a) to (j) with side couples leading. (88 bars)

(l) All couples repeat (a) and (b). (16 bars)

FIGURE 4: JIG (184 BARS)

(a) All couples dance around the house using the shunting movement – the ladies reverse all round as the gents dance forward. (8 bars)

(b) All couples house around. (8 bars)

(c) Both top couples dance at home, turning once in place. (8 bars)

(d) Starting with the lady on their right and finishing with their own partners, the top gents swing with each lady in turn. (32 bars)

(e) Top couples house around each other. (8 bars)

(f) All gents swing the lady on their left, then swing their partners. (16 bars)

(g) Repeat (a) to (f) with side couples leading. (80 bars)

(h) All couples repeat (a) and (b). (16 bars)

FIGURE 5 : REEL (256 BARS)

(a) All couples lead around holding crossed hands and turn the lady. (8 bars)

(b) Linking left arms, all dance around their partners, turning twice. (8 bars)

(c) All couples swing. (8 bars)

(d) Top couples square anticlockwise all round the centre, dancing 'sevens' along each side of the square. (8 bars)

(e) Top couples house around each other. (8 bars)

(f) Top gents cross (2 bars) and swing the opposite lady (6 bars). (8 bars)

(g) Top gents link left arms in the centre and dance around each other, then return to their own partners. (8 bars)

(h) Repeat (a) to (g) with side couples leading. (56 bars)

(i) Repeat (a) to (h) with all couples dancing again. (112 bars)

(j) All dance (a), (b) and (c) again. (24 bars)

MULLAHORAN SET

This set was revived by Antóin MacGabhann with a group of dancers from the Mullahoran area in Cavan. It was taught to me by Josie O'Rourke of Mullahoran on a couple of occasions and we danced it in Drumshanbo in July 1998 under Josie's guidance. All swing for six bars and dance out the last two throughout the set. The jig and polka figures are danced to the 'polka' step (1 2 3). The reel figures are danced to the Cavan reel step. (The basic step is 'batter' 1 2 3.)

FIGURE 1: JIG (104 BARS) – INTRODUCTION

(a) Top ladies chain with right hands in the centre, hook left arm with opposite gent to turn around him and dance back to home.   (8 bars)

(b) Top couples dance free, facing their partners.   (8 bars)

(c) Top couples swing in *céilí* hold.   (8 bars)

(d) Top couples dance (a) to (c).   (24 bars)

(e) Side couples dance (a) to (d), with top couples swinging as well the last time.   (48 bars)

FIGURE 2: REEL (160 BARS) – COURTSHIP

(a) All advance and retire twice in a circle.   (8 bars)

(b) All couples dance free and swing in place.   (16 bars)

(c) Top couples take right hands and turn anticlockwise twice as they cross anticlockwise to opposite positions (4 bars), then dance free there, partners facing each other (4 bars).   (8 bars)

(d) Top couples repeat (c), dancing clockwise back to home, turning anticlockwise again.   (8 bars)

(e) Top couples swing.   (8 bars)

(f) Top couples take right hands and turn anticlockwise twice as they cross clockwise to opposite positions (4 bars), then dance free there, partners facing each other (4 bars).   (8 bars)

(g) Top couples repeat (c), dancing anticlockwise to home, turning anticlockwise again.   (8 bars)

(h) All advance and retire twice in a circle.   (8 bars)

(i) All couples dance free (8 bars) and swing in place.   (16 bars)

(j) Repeat (c) to (h) with side couples leading.   (64 bars)

FIGURE 3: REEL (168 BARS) – MARRYING

(a) Top lady and opposite gent dance across, passing right shoulder to right, and reverse back, passing left shoulder to left, to face each other in the centre. (8 bars)

(b) Top lady and opposite gent swing (6 bars), then reverse back to their own partners (2 bars). (8 bars)

(c) Top couples take right hand in right, dance clockwise around the opposite couple, turning three times, and dance out the last two bars at home. (8 bars)

(d) Top couples dance out facing their partners. (8 bars)

(e) Top couples swing. (8 bars)

(f) Side couples repeat (a) to (e), with the first lady (on the left) and the second gent leading. (40 bars)

(g) Top couples repeat (a) to (e). This time the top gent and the second top lady lead. (40 bars)

(h) Side couples repeat (a) to (e). This time the first side gent and the second side lady lead. Top couples dance (d) and (e) along with side couples the second time. (40 bars)

FIGURE 4: REEL (168 BARS) – BLESSING

(a) Top ladies chain with right hands in the centre, hook left arm with opposite gent to turn around him and dance back to home. (8 bars)

(b) Top couples dance free, facing their partners. (8 bars)

(c) Top couples swing in *céilí* hold. (8 bars)

(d) Top couples take right hand in right. Both couples advance and retire, then advance again. As his own partner turns in to face him, the top gent takes the opposite lady's left hand in his left. Both gents now retire, both ladies going with the top gent and turning in slightly – the top lady clockwise and the second lady anticlockwise – to stand beside him in the first top position. (8 bars)

(e) All advance and retire, then advance again. Both ladies give their free hands to the second gent and, as both gents retire, they dance with the second gent to the second top position and turn in beside him, the top lady anticlockwise and the second lady clockwise.

(8 bars)

(f) All four advance and retire again, then advance to form a circle of four in the centre, ladies facing in to place their hands on the gents' shoulders. (8 bars)

(g) Top couples swing in four in the centre. (8 bars)

(h) Top ladies chain again. (8 bars)

(i) Top couples dance free, then swing their partners. (16 bars)

(j) Side couples repeat, all dancing (i) the last time. (80 bars)

FIGURE 5: POLKA (88 BARS) – OFFERING UP

(a) All advance and retire twice in a circle.   (8 bars)

(b) Top ladies chain, followed two bars behind by side ladies.   (8 bars)

(c) All couples dance anticlockwise around the house, stepping in
and back, with the ladies reversing all the time, as in the
'shunting' danced in some Munster sets. In the opposite position,
all ladies turn clockwise under their partner's hand during the
seventh and eight bars. They then continue anticlockwise to
home, with the ladies turning again during the last two bars.

(16 bars)

(d) Repeat (a) to (c) with top ladies leading the chain again.   (32 bars)

(e) All advance and retire twice in a circle.   (8 bars)

(f) All couples swing in place.   (8 bars)

FIGURE 6: REEL (96 BARS) – WEDDING PARTY

(a) All advance and retire twice in a circle.   (8 bars)

(b) All couples dance free in place.   (8 bars)

(c) All couples lead around, arms around their partner's back.   (8 bars)

(d) Ladies dance on, passing inside and turning anticlockwise slightly
to face the next gent on the right, then all dance free, facing their
new partners.   (8 bars)

(e) Repeat (c) and (d) until ladies are back home.   (48 bars)

(f) All advance and retire twice in a circle.   (8 bars)

NEDINAGH SET

This set was first described to me by Pete Brett from Philadelphia, who visited the Joe Mooney Summer School in Drumshanbo. It had been danced for many years by Irish–American dancers; Pete sent me their notes on the set, as written by Jean Ver Hoeven. A few years later, Pete and I met again, and he put me in touch with Jean, who described the set to me in detail and provided a video recording of it; these notes are based on that recording. In the set, the first side couple are on the right-hand side of the first top couple.

FIGURE 1: (THE ARCHES) POLKA (240 BARS)

(a) First top couple dance on the spot, with the lady reversing slightly (2 bars), then house around inside to second side position (6 bars), moving in from the left (gent's) side of the side couple. (8 bars)

(b) As the first top couple move in on their left, the second side couple move out, with the lady reversing (2 bars), and house inside as the first top couple had done, to finish in the second top position (6 bars). (8 bars)

(c) Second top couple move out and repeat the house, finishing in first side position. (8 bars)

(d) First side couple move out and repeat the house, finishing in first top position. (8 bars)

(e) As the second top couple take inside hands, the first top lady crosses the set, giving her right hand to the second top gent's left and the three of them dance the arches, or monkey chain. The first top lady goes under the arch first, followed by the gent. Then the second top lady goes under the arch, again followed by the gent. Finally, the first top lady goes under the arch a second time, again followed by the gent. (8 bars)

(f) With all three of them still holding hands, the first top lady leads the second top couple under an arch made by the second side couple, who face them as they start towards the arch. They continue until they reach the first top position, where the second couple stay, while the first top lady takes her own partner's nearest hand and follows him under an arch made by the first side couple to the second top position. (8 bars)

(g) Both top couples house across to their own positions (4 bars), then all four couples swing in place in waltz hold (4 bars). (8 bars)

(h) All repeat (a) to (d) with the first top couple leading off again. (32 bars)

(i) Top couples repeat (e) and (f), the second top lady dancing the arches with the first top couple and leading them under the arch.(16 bars)

(j) Both top couples house across to their own positions (4 bars), then all four couples swing in place in waltz hold (4 bars).   (8 bars)

(k) All repeat (a) to (d) with the first top couple leading off again.

    (32 bars)

(l) Side couples dance (e) and (f), the first side lady dancing the arches with the second side couple and leading them under the arch.   (16 bars)

(m) Both side couples house across to their own positions (4 bars), then all four couples swing in place in waltz hold (4 bars).   (8 bars)

(n) All repeat (a) to (d) with the first top couple leading off again. (32 bars)

(o) Side couples repeat (e) and (f), the second side lady dancing the arches with the first side couple and leading them under the arch.

    (16 bars)

(p) Both side couples house across to their own positions (4 bars), then all four couples swing in place in waltz hold (4 bars).   (8 bars)

(q) All couples swing in waltz hold.   (8 bars)

FIGURE 2: (THE CHASE) POLKA (104 BARS)

(a) First top couple house around inside to second side position, going around second side couple, while second side couple, starting two bars behind them, house around to second top position.   (8 bars)

(b) Second top couple house around inside to first side position, going around first side couple, while first side couple, starting two bars behind them, house around to the vacant first top position. During the last two bars, all dance on the spot (1 bar) and the gents 'lift' the ladies, who jump (1 bar).   (8 bars)

(c) Repeat (a) and (b), all couples moving on another position, to finish in the position opposite their own.   (16 bars)

(d) The four ladies dance a chain inside, top ladies going to their left and side ladies going to their right. All begin by giving their right hand to the first lady they meet, then their left hand to the next lady. They continue around, giving their right hand and left hand again to get back home.   (8 bars)

(e) The four gents dance a chain inside, top gents going to their left and side gents going to their right. All begin by giving their right hand to the first gent they meet, then their left hand to the next gent. They continue around, giving their right hand and left hand again to get back home. (8 bars)

(f) Top couples chain around inside. They give their right hands to
the opposite person, their left to their own partner, their right to
the opposite person again and their left to their own partner as
they dance back into their own positions. (8 bars)

(g) Side couples chain around inside. They give their right hands to
the opposite person, their left to their own partner, their right to
the opposite person again and their left to their own partner as
they dance back into their own positions. (8 bars)

(h) All repeat (a), (b) and (c). (32 bars)

FIGURE 3: HORNPIPE (104 BARS)

(a) All couples take crossed hands and face into the set. They step to
the right (hop 1 2 3), back to the left (hop 1 2 3), then double
clockwise in place (hop 1, hop 2, hop 3, hop 4). They now step to
the left (hop 1 2 3), back to the right (hop 1 2 3) and double turn
clockwise in place again. (8 bars)

(b) From the second double, the first top couple finish facing the wall
– out of their own position, with the lady on the right-hand side of
the gent. The first side couple (on their right) now dance into line
behind them and the second side couple dance into line third,
while the second top couple are fourth in line (2 bars). Breaking
from the wall, the four ladies face the four gents and the two lines
retire (2 bars), then advance again (2 bars), and, taking their
partners in waltz hold, all dance one double in place in line, in the
same order as when they stood facing the wall (2 bars). (8 bars)

(c) Keeping this order, all couples now house around, the first top
couple followed by the first side couple, the second side couple
and the second top couple, who finish on the right of the first tops
when they all face into the set again. (8 bars)

(d) All couples dance (a). This time, the second top couple face out to
lead the wall. (8 bars)

(e) As the second top couple stand facing out in the position on the
right, the second side couple dance in behind them, the first top
couple dance into the third position and the first side couple line
up fourth (2 bars). Again, each lady is on the right of her partner.
Breaking from the wall, the four ladies face the four gents and the
two lines retire (2 bars), then advance again (2 bars), and, taking
their partners in waltz hold, all dance one double in place in line,
in the same order as when they stood facing the wall (2 bars). (8 bars)

(f) All couples house around again, the second top couple followed by the second side couple, the first top couple and the first side couple. (8 bars)

(g) All couples dance (a). This time, the first side couple face out to lead the wall, in the second top couple's original position. (8 bars)

(h) As the first side couple face out of the second top position, the first top couple (on their right) line up behind them, followed by the second top couple, with the second side couple fourth in line (2 bars). Breaking from the wall, the four ladies face the four gents and the two lines retire (2 bars), then advance again (2 bars), and, taking their partners in waltz hold, all dance one double in place in line, in the same order as when they stood facing the wall (2 bars). (8 bars)

(i) All couples house, the first side couple followed by the first top couple the second top couple and the second side couple. (8 bars)

(j) All couples dance (a). This time, the second side couple face out to lead the wall, in their own original position. (8 bars)

(k) As the second side couple face the wall, the second top couple (on their right) line up behind them, with the first side couple third and the first top couple fourth (2 bars). Breaking from the wall, the four ladies face the four gents and the two lines retire (2 bars), then advance again (2 bars), and, taking their partners in waltz hold, all dance one double in place in line, in the same order as when they stood facing the wall (2 bars). (8 bars)

(l) All couples house, the second side couple followed by the second top couple, the first side couple and the first top couple. All now finish back in their own places. (8 bars)

FIGURE 4: POLKA (200 BARS)

(a) First top couple house around inside, finishing in front of the second side couple, who dance the last two bars on the spot. (8 bars)

(b) First top couple now house again, followed by the second side couple. The first top couple finish in the second side position and the second side couple finish in front of the second top couple, who dance the last two bars on the spot. (8 bars)

(c) Second side couple now house again, followed by the second top couple. First side couple finish in the second top position and the second top couple finish in front of the first side couple, who dance the last two bars on the spot. (8 bars)

(d) Second top couple now house again, followed by the first side

138

couple. The second top couple finish in the first side position and the first side couple finish in the first top position. (8 bars)

(e) First side couple house again, finishing in the first top position, and all couples dance in and back during the last two bars. (8 bars)

(f) All gents advance and raise joined hands in the centre, then retire. Ladies repeat. (8 bars)

(g) Repeat (a) to (e), the first top couple leading again. (40 bars)

(h) All gents join right hands in the centre, dancing all the way round to home, then ladies join left hands in the centre, again dancing all the way around to home. (8 bars)

(i) Repeat (a) to (e), the first top couple leading again. (40 bars)

(j) All gents dance anticlockwise around the lady on their right, coming back behind their own partners into place. (8 bars)

(k) All ladies dance anticlockwise around the gent on their left, coming back behind their own partners into place. (8 bars)

(l) Repeat (a) to (e), the first top couple leading again. (40 bars)

PRIDE OF ERIN WALTZ

This beautiful waltz is danced in many parts of Ireland, particularly at céilithe in the North of Ireland. Slightly different versions of it are danced from place to place. All couples start the dance facing around the room anticlockwise, with ladies on the right-hand side of their partners.

(a) Holding near hands, step forward on the outside foot, swinging the other foot forward, then step back on the inside foot, pointing the outside toe in front. (2 bars)

(b) Dance forward, starting on the outside foot – 1 (pause), 2, 3 (turning to face back on three). (2 bars)

(c) Dance (a) and (b) in the opposite direction, all turning in to face partner and taking both hands on '3'. (4 bars)

(d) Bring the back foot (gent's left, lady's right) across in front of the other one, then bring the other foot (gent's right, lady's left) across behind and point the toe, tapping the floor. (2 bars)

(e) Dance (d) the other way, bringing the other foot across in front. (2 bars)

(f) Dance two turns, turning out from partner, (gent anticlockwise, lady clockwise), moving in an anticlockwise direction. Touch near hands (gent's right, lady's left) after the first turn. (4 bars)

(g) Take both hands wide at shoulder height. Take both hands wide at shoulder height facing each other, right hand in partner's left. Advance left shoulder to left, stepping on the right foot and swinging the left foot forward, then step back on the left foot, pointing the right toe. (2 bars)

(h) Change sides, with the lady turning clockwise under her partner's left arm, crossing and turning anticlockwise until right around, to face each other from the other side. (2 bars)

(i) Repeat (g) and (h), starting from the opposite side and crossing back to the first side again. (4 bars)

(j) All face around the room anticlockwise in waltz hold, with gents turned slightly towards the wall and ladies towards the centre. With the gent starting on the left foot and the lady starting on the right, all dance (slide) 1, 2, 3, forward (2 bars) and repeat, sliding back (2 bars). (4 bars)

(k) Waltz, turning clockwise twice. (4 bars)

(l) Repeat (a) to (k) while the music lasts.

Roscahill Set

This set comes from Roscahill near Oughterard in County Galway. It was taught by Marie Philbin at the Galway International Set Dancing Weekend in 1996. Marie learned the set from her father.

Figure 1: Polka (200 bars)

(a) Facing into the set, all couples advance and retire twice in waltz hold. The steps are: tap 1 2 3, tap 1 2 3 when advancing and retiring. (8 bars)

(b) All couples house across to opposite positions, turning three times, then dance out facing into the set at the other side. (8 bars)

(c) All couples repeat (a) and (b), dancing back to home. (16 bars)

(d) Top ladies chain with right hands in the centre, turn with left hand around the opposite gent, holding hands around waist height, and chain back to place. (8 bars)

(e) All couples swing in place (6 bars) and dance out (2 bars). (8 bars)

(f) Side ladies chain. (8 bars)

(g) All couples swing again and dance out. (8 bars)

(h) Top couples advance and retire once in waltz hold, then advance into a line of four, with each lady between the opposite couple and the gents on the outside, all still facing forward from their own positions (8 bars). Each dancer now turns clockwise once, right arm in right, with the opposite lady or gent, then all turn anticlockwise one and a half times around their own partner, left arm in left as they dance into opposite positions (8 bars). (16 bars)

(i) Top couples repeat (h), starting in opposite positions and dancing back to home. (16 bars)

(j) Side couples dance (h) and (i). (32 bars)

(k) All ladies dance to the gent on the left (2 bars) and swing with him (6 bars), then move on to each other gent and swing until back swinging their partners. (32 bars)

(l) All repeat (a), (b) and (c) to finish the figure. (32 bars)

Figure 2: Jig (112 bars)

(a) In waltz hold, all couples dance one step in to the centre, one step back and turn clockwise to the position on the right (4 bars), then repeat the movements three times, dancing around the set to home (12 bars). (16 bars)

(b) All couples swing in place. (8 bars)

(c) Top ladies cross to opposite positions, passing right shoulder to right (4 bars), then side ladies cross to opposite positions (4 bars).

(8 bars)

(d) Taking their new partners in waltz hold, all couples dance one step to the centre and back, then top couples house around the side couple on their right. (8 bars)

(e) Ladies cross back (8 bars) and all repeat (d), this time all dancing with their own partners. Top couples dance to their right again. (16 bars)

(f) The four gents join right hands in the centre, dance around clockwise, then join left hands and dance back to place. (8 bars)

(g) Keeping left hands in the centre, gents place their right arm over their partner's shoulder, taking her right hand in his right, and lead around anticlockwise to home, bringing the right hand forward over the lady's head as they arrive there. (8 bars)

(h) All couples swing in place. (8 bars)

(i) All couples repeat (a) and (b) to finish. (24 bars)

FIGURE 3: POLKA (96 BARS)

(a) All advance and retire twice, holding hands in a circle. (8 bars)

(b) Back to back: facing their partners, all dance forward, passing left shoulder to left (4 bars), then reverse back to place, passing right shoulder to right (4 bars). (8 bars)

(c) All advance and retire in the circle again. (8 bars)

(d) All couples swing in place. (8 bars)

(e) Taking their partner's right hand to begin, all chain around the set, gents dancing anticlockwise and ladies clockwise. When partners meet in opposite positions, they dance out the last bar of the first eight holding right hands, then continue the chain back to place. (16 bars)

(f) All couples swing in place. (8 bars)

(g) All advance and retire in a circle. (8 bars)

(h) Facing their partners, all dance the back-to-back again. (8 bars)

(i) Holding hands in a circle, all advance and retire once, then advance again and link arms behind each other's backs. (8 bars)

(j) All swing in the circle of eight to finish the set. (8 bars)

ROYAL COTILLION

*Versions of this dance have been published in a number
of old dance manuals.*

FIGURE 1: WALTZ (136 BARS OR 264 BARS)

(a) All couples waltz around the house and turn the lady.   (16 bars)

(b) First top couple house inside twice.   (16 bars)

(c) Top ladies waltz across, then top gents waltz across.   (8 bars)

(d) Side ladies waltz across, then side gents waltz across.   (8 bars)

(e) All take right hands with the person in the corner. Balance
forward and back, then gents turn the ladies into the ladies' own
places (4 bars). All now take their own partner's right hand,
balance again, and gents turn the lady into place, taking waltz
hold (4 bars).   (8 bars)

(f) All couples waltz around to their own places.   (8 bars)

(g) Repeat (a) to (f) three times, the second top couple and both side
couples leading in turn. First side couple are on the right.
Alternatively, (a) to (f) can be danced twice, top couples dancing
(b) together the first time and side couples dancing (b) together
the second time.

FIGURE 2: WALTZ (104 BARS OR 200 BARS)

(a) Top couples advance with waltz steps to the centre, join right
hands and dance across, then turn, join left hands and dance back
to place.   (8 bars)

(b) Side couples dance (a).   (8 bars)

(c) All take hands in a circle, balance forward and back (2 bars), then
ladies waltz on to the gent on the right (2 bars). This movement is
repeated three times, ladies moving around the set to
their own places.   (16 bars)

(d) All couples waltz around the house.   (16 bars)

(e) Repeat (a) to (d) with side couples leading.   (48 bars)

(f) Repeat (a) to (e) if desired.   (96 bars)

FIGURE 3: WALTZ (136 BARS OR 264 BARS)

(a) Chain all round, ladies clockwise and gents anticlockwise. From the
chain, all dance into lines of four in top positions, with side dancers
facing their own partners on the outside of each line.   (16 bars)

(b) The lines advance and retire once (4 bars), then pass through, right shoulder to right with the opposite person, to the other side.

(8 bars)

(c) Repeat (b) from the other side, crossing back to place.   (8 bars)

(d) Taking their own partners right hand in right, all dance one full turn (4 bars), then pass each other forward, taking left hand in left with the next lady or gent (2 bars).   (6 bars)

(e) Repeat (d), turning around this person with left hand in left and moving on to take right hands with the next person.   (6 bars)

(f) Repeat (d) and (e) with the next two dancers, all meeting their own partners at the opposite side of the set.   (12 bars)

(g) All couples waltz around to home.   (8 bars)

(h) Repeat (a) to (g), lining up in side positions from the chain.   (64 bars)

(i) Dance (a) to (h) again if desired.   (128 bars)

SEIT DOIRE CHOLMCILLE

This set was composed by Frank Roddy of Derry some years ago. Music for the set was recorded by Matt Cunningham during Easter 1999. Thanks to Anne O'Donnell for her help in teaching me the set and to Frank Roddy for his notes and advice.

FIGURE 1: REEL (128 BARS)

(a) All couples lead around holding crossed hands. Each lady turns clockwise under her partner's raised hands during the last two bars. (8 bars)

(b) All couples swing in waltz hold. (8 bars)

(c) Top couples house around each other. (8 bars)

(d) Top couples face the side couple on their left. All pass through, with ladies in the centre, and reverse back with gents in the centre (4 bars), then the four dancers join right hands and dance a full turn clockwise back to their own places (4 bars). (8 bars)

(e) All couples swing in waltz hold. (8 bars)

(f) Side couples house around each other. (8 bars)

(g) All repeat (d) with side couples turning left and top couples turning right. (8 bars)

(h) All couples swing in waltz hold. (8 bars)

(i) All repeat (c) to (h). (48 bars)

(j) All couples house around. (8 bars)

FIGURE 2: REEL (160 BARS)

(a) All couples lead around holding crossed hands. Each lady turns clockwise under her partner's raised hands during the last two bars. (8 bars)

(b) All couples swing in waltz hold. (8 bars)

(c) Top couples house around each other. (8 bars)

(d) Top couples advance and retire once, holding inside hands (4 bars), then the first top couple form an arch and the second gent crosses under the arch to the first top gent's position while the second lady moves forward, giving her right hand to the top gent's left (4 bars). (8 bars)

(e) Top gent and the two ladies dance the arches or high gates. The first top lady passes under the arch first, then the second top lady and, finally, the first top lady again. During the last two bars, the three of them face the second top gent and form a group of four in the centre. (8 bars)

(f) Top couples swing in four in the centre (6 bars) and reverse to place (2 bars). (8 bars)

(g) Side couples dance (c) to (f). The first side couple, on the left of the first top couple, lead. (32 bars)

(h) Repeat (c) to (g). This time, the second top couple and the second side couple lead. (64 bars)

(i) All couples house around. (8 bars)

FIGURE 3: REEL (144 BARS)

(a) All couples lead around holding crossed hands. Each lady turns clockwise under her partner's raised hands during the last two bars. (8 bars)

(b) All couples swing in waltz hold. (8 bars)

(c) Top ladies chain with right hands in the centre, turn with left arms around the opposite gent and chain with right hands again as they dance back to place. (8 bars)

(d) Top couples house around each other. (8 bars)

(e) Top couples face the side couple on their left, all holding inside hands. They advance and retire once, then change places, top couples forming an arch and side couples passing under the arch (4 bars). They repeat the movements three times as they dance around the set to home. Top couples move left each time and side couples move right. (32 bars)

(f) All couples swing in place. (8 bars)

(g) All repeat (c) to (f) with side couples leading. They turn left at (e) and form the arch. (56 bars)

(h) All couples house around. (8 bars)

FIGURE 4: JIG (104 BARS)

(a) All couples lead around holding crossed hands. Each lady turns clockwise under her partner's raised hands during the last two bars. (8 bars)

(b) All couples swing in waltz hold. (8 bars)

(c) All couples house around. (8 bars)

(d) All gents advance (1 2 3, 1 2 3) and retire once while ladies dance on the spot (1 2 3, 1 2 3), then dance to the position on the right and turn clockwise to face the next gent (4 bars). All couples, with new partners, dance halfway around the set from where they are (4 bars). (8 bars)

(e) All couples swing. (8 bars)

(f) All repeat (d) and (e) three times until swinging their partners
at home. (48 bars)

(g) All couples house around. (8 bars)

FIGURE 5: HORNPIPE (152 BARS)

(a) Taking hands in a circle, all couples advance and retire once, then
dance at home, turning once. During the last two bars, ladies turn
clockwise under their partner's left hand and move to join the next
gent on their left. (8 bars)

(b) All dance on the spot with their new partners (2 bars), then double
to the next position on their right (2 bars). They repeat these
movements three times until back in the gents' own original
positions (12 bars). (16 bars)

(c) All couples dance around the house. (8 bars)

(d) The dancers repeat (a) to (c) until all house with their own
partners again. (96 bars)

(e) Taking hands in a circle again, all advance and retire once, then
dance at home. (8 bars)

(f) All couples house around. (8 bars)

SET OF ERIN

This gentle set from west Cork has been made popular by dancing teacher Timmy McCarthy.

FIGURE 1: SLIDE (184 BARS)

(a) Dancing a polka step, all four couples lead around anticlockwise, each gent's arm around his partner's waist and her left hand on his shoulder. (8 bars)

(b) All couples dance around the house. (8 bars)

(c) First top couple 'show the lady' (house inside). (8 bars)

(d) All couples slide to the centre and back, each gent's arm around the lady's waist (4 bars), then all gents move to their left and swing one turn with the lady there. (8 bars)

(e) Repeat (d) three more times, all advancing with each new partner and gents moving to their left each time until they finish back at home swinging their own partners. (24 bars)

(f) Dance (c) to (e) three more times, with first side couple (on the left of first top couple), second top couple and second side couple leading in turn. (120 bars)

FIGURE 2: SLIDES (184 BARS)

(a) Dancing a polka step, all four couples lead around anticlockwise, each gent's arm around his partner's waist and her left hand on his shoulder. (8 bars)

(b) All couples dance around the house. (8 bars)

(c) First top couple show the lady (house inside). (8 bars)

(d) All couples slide to the centre and back, with the gent's arm around the lady's waist (4 bars), then all ladies move to their left and swing with the gent there, turning once in place. (8 bars)

(e) Repeat (d) three more times, all advancing with each new partner and ladies moving to their left each time until they finish back at home swinging their own partners. (24 bars)

(f) Dance (c) to (e) three more times, with first side couple (on the left of first top couple), second top couple and second side couple leading in turn. (120 bars)

FIGURE 3: SLIDES (184 BARS)

(a) Dancing a polka step, all four couples lead around anticlockwise, each gent's arm around his partner's waist and her left hand on his shoulder. (8 bars)

(b) All couples dance around the house. (8 bars)

(c) First top couple 'show the lady' (house inside). (8 bars)

(d) All couples slide to the centre and back, each gent's arm around the lady's waist (4 bars), then top gents cross, passing right shoulder to right, and turn once in place with opposite top ladies.
(8 bars)

(e) All couples slide to the centre and back, each gent's arm around the lady's waist (4 bars), then top gents turn to their left and turn once in place with the side lady there. (8 bars)

(f) Top gents and side ladies slide to the centre and back, each gent's arm around the lady's waist, then top gents cross, passing right shoulder to right, and turn once in place with opposite side ladies.
(8 bars)

(g) Top gents and side ladies slide to the centre and back, each gent's arm around the lady's waist, then top gents dance to their right and turn once in place with their own partners. (8 bars)

(h) First side couple 'show the lady' (house inside). (8 bars)

(i) All couples slide to the centre and back, each gent's arm around the lady's waist (4 bars), then side gents cross, passing right shoulder to right, and turn once in place with opposite side ladies.
(8 bars)

(j) All couples slide to the centre and back, each gent's arm around the lady's waist (4 bars), then side gents turn to their left and turn once in place with the top lady there. (8 bars)

(k) Side gents and top ladies slide to the centre and back, each gent's arm around the lady's waist, then side gents cross, passing right shoulder to right, and turn once in place with opposite top ladies.
(8 bars)

(l) Side gents and top ladies slide to the centre and back, each gent's arm around the lady's waist, then side gents dance to their right and turn once in place with their own partners. (8 bars)

(m) Repeat (c) to (g) with second top couple dancing (c) and top couples leading. (40 bars)

(n) Repeat (h) to (l) with second side couple dancing (c) and side couples leading. (40 bars)

FIGURE 4: SLIDES (184 BARS)

(a) Dancing a polka step, all four couples lead around anticlockwise,

149

each gent's arm around his partner's waist and her left hand on his shoulder. (8 bars)

(b) All couples dance around the house. (8 bars)

(c) First top couple 'show the lady' (house inside). (8 bars)

(d) All couples slide to the centre and back with each gent's arm around the lady's waist (4 bars), then top gents cross, passing right shoulder to right, and turn once in place with opposite top ladies, while side gents cross immediately after them and turn once in place with opposite side ladies. (8 bars)

(e) All couples slide to the centre and back, each gent's arm around the lady's waist (4 bars), then all gents turn once in place with the lady on their left. Top gents are now with side ladies, while side gents are with top ladies. (8 bars)

(f) All couples slide to the centre and back, each gent's arm around the lady's waist (4 bars), then top gents cross, passing right shoulder to right, and turn once in place with opposite side ladies, while side gents cross immediately after them and turn once in place with opposite top ladies. (8 bars)

(g) All couples slide to the centre and back, each gent's arm around the lady's waist (4 bars), then all gents dance to their right and turn once in place with their own partners. (8 bars)

(h) First side couple 'show the lady' (house inside). (8 bars)

(i) All couples slide to the centre and back, each gent's arm around the lady's waist (4 bars), then side gents cross, passing right shoulder to right, and turn once in place with opposite side ladies, while top gents cross immediately after them and turn once in place with opposite top ladies. (8 bars)

(j) All couples slide to the centre and back, each gent's arm around the lady's waist (4 bars), then all gents turn once in place with the lady on their left. Top gents are now with side ladies, while side gents are with top ladies. (8 bars)

(k) All couples slide to the centre and back, each gent's arm around the lady's waist (4 bars), then side gents cross, passing right shoulder to right, and turn once in place with opposite top ladies, while top gents cross immediately after them and turn once in place with opposite side ladies. (8 bars)

(l) All couples slide to the centre and back, each gent's arm around the lady's waist (4 bars), then all gents dance to their right and turn once in place with their own partners. (8 bars)

(m) Repeat (c) to (g) with second top couple dancing (c) and top couples leading. (40 bars)

150

(n) Repeat (h) to (l) with second side couple dancing (c) and side
   couples leading. (40 bars)

FIGURE 5: SLIDE (120 BARS)

(a) Top couples house around each other. (8 bars)
(b) Top couples square forward across the set, reverse through
   opposite positions (4 bars) and house back to home positions
   (4 bars). (8 bars)
(c) Top couples square forward across the set, reverse through
   opposite positions (4 bars) and house back to home positions
   (4 bars). (8 bars)
(d) Top couples house around each other. (8 bars)
(e) Top couples repeat (b) to (d). (24 bars)
(f) Side couples dance (a) to (e). (56 bars)

FIGURE 6: REEL (272 BARS)

(a) All couples lead around, holding crossed hands in front. (8 bars)
(b) Facing their partners, the gents turn the ladies clockwise, left hand
   in left hand, four times (8 bars), then all couples swing (8 bars).(16 bars)
(c) Top couples square anticlockwise all round the centre, dancing
   'sevens' along each side of the square. (8 bars)
(d) Top couples house around each other. (8 bars)
(e) Top gents cross (2 bars) and swing the opposite lady (6 bars). (8 bars)
(f) Top gents link left arms in the centre and dance around each other
   (6 bars), then double around each other (2 bars), breaking away to
   their own partners from the double. (8 bars)
(g) Repeat (a) to (f) with side couples leading. (56 bars)
(h) Repeat (a) to (g) with all couples dancing again. (112 bars)
(i) All dance (a) and (b) again. (24 bars)
(j) All couples dance the 'diamond' square – dancing 'sevens' all
   around the house. (8 bars)
(k) All couples house around. (8 bars)

SHRAMORE SET

As described by dancing teacher Ciarán Condron of Dublin. Ciarán learned the set from Mickey Kelly and the Newport Dancers from County Mayo. I was given further help with the set by Mickey Kelly.

FIGURE 1: JIG (320 BARS)

(a) Top couples square – dance to face the side couple on their left, reverse into the position opposite their own, dance to face the couple on their left and reverse to home positions. (8 bars)

(b) Top couples swing in *céilí* hold. (8 bars)

(c) Top ladies chain – right hands in the centre, left arm to opposite gent and dance back to place, passing right shoulder to right. (8 bars)

(d) Top couples pass across on the right, ladies leading, holding the gent's right hand in their left, and lead back on the same side. (8 bars)

(e) Side couples dance (a) to (d). (32 bars)

(f) All dancers turn to place their hands on the waist of the dancer on their left, forming a circle or ring of dancers. In this formation, they dance slowly clockwise around the set, ladies stepping onto the left foot and battering on the right, while gents step onto the right foot and batter on the left. (16 bars)

(g) All couples swing in place. (8 bars)

(h) All couples repeat (f) and (g). (24 bars)

(i) Top gent and opposite lady swing in the centre (6 bars), reversing back to place. (8 bars)

(j) Top couples pass across and back on the right-hand side, ladies leading, with their left hand in the gent's right. (8 bars)

(k) Top lady and opposite gent swing in the centre. (8 bars)

(l) Top couples pass across and back on the right-hand side again. (8 bars)

(m) Top ladies chain with right hands in the centre and left arm around the opposite gent and dance back to face their own partner as he faces into the set. (8 bars)

(n) Top couples turn anticlockwise in place, then the gents reverse the lady across on the right and turn clockwise into opposite positions. (8 bars)

(o) Top couples repeat (n), dancing back to home. (8 bars)

(p) Top couples swing in four in the centre, arms around the waist. (8 bars)

(q) Top couples repeat (m) to (p). (32 bars)

(r) Side couples dance (i) to (q). (96 bars)

(s) All couples swing to finish. (8 bars)

FIGURE 2: POLKA (200 BARS)

(a) Top couples dance 'sevens' across the set, gents passing back to back. They dance fourteen steps on the way over, with gents starting by stepping onto the left foot and ladies onto the right. Changing weight to the other foot, they dance sevens back to place, ladies passing back to back this time.   (8 bars)

(b) Top couples house around each other.   (8 bars)

(c) Top couples repeat (a) and (b).   (16 bars)

(d) Top ladies chain.   (8 bars)

(e) Top couples swing in place in waltz hold.   (8 bars)

(f) Side couples dance (a) to (e).   (48 bars)

(g) Repeat (a) to (f), with all couples swinging the last time.   (96 bars)

FIGURE 3: REEL (184 BARS)

(a) Holding hands in a circle, all advance and retire twice.   (8 bars)

(b) Ladies join right hands in the centre and dance around clockwise, then join left hands and dance back, passing outside their own partners into their own places.   (8 bars)

(c) Gents join right hands in the centre and dance around, then join left hands and dance back to place.   (8 bars)

(d) All swing their partners in waltz hold.   (8 bars)

(e) Each gent places his right arm around the lady's waist as she places her hand on his shoulder, and all lead around clockwise, ladies on the inside.   (8 bars)

(f) Ladies join right hands in the centre and dance around clockwise, then join left hands and dance back, passing inside their own partners and outside the next gent to move on to the position to the right of their own.   (8 bars)

(g) Gents join right hands in the centre, dance around, then join left hands and dance back.   (8 bars)

(h) All swing their partners in waltz hold.   (8 bars)

(i) Each gent places his right arm around the lady's waist as she places her hand on his shoulder, and all lead around.   (8 bars)

(j) All repeat (f) to (i) until leading around with their own partners.(96 bars)

(k) Circle, advance and retire twice to finish.   (8 bars)

SLIGO SET

This set was taught by Sligo dancing teacher Brenda O'Callaghan at the O'Carolan Harp Festival in Keadue in 1997.

FIGURE 1: REEL (248 BARS)

(a) All lead around in the 'lock' hold, gents with their left hand on the shoulder of the gent on their right (in front of them in the lock) and holding their partner's right hand in their right, dancing on the spot in each position. They turn the lady during the last two bars.

(16 bars)

(b) Top couples form a circle of four with the side couple on their right. They dance around clockwise (4 bars), then the side couple dance anticlockwise back to place, passing under the arch made by the top couple (4 bars). During the last two bars, the top couple turn under their own arch, the lady anticlockwise and the gent clockwise, into their own places.

(8 bars)

(c) Taking her right hand in his left, gents turn the lady on their left clockwise twice (4 bars). They then take their own partner's left hand in their right and turn her anticlockwise twice, dancing in place all the time (4 bars).

(8 bars)

(d) All couples swing in waltz hold.

(8 bars)

(e) First top lady dances anticlockwise around inside, then turns clockwise and dances clockwise back to place. While she is doing this, the other dancers form a circle around her and dance around clockwise (4 bars), then dance back to place anticlockwise (4 bars).

(8 bars)

(f) Top lady finishes facing her partner as he faces in and she faces out. They dance on the spot (4 bars), then swing (4 bars).

(8 bars)

(g) The lady dances from the swing to face the opposite top gent, repeats the dance on the spot and swings with him. This time the lady finishes with her back to the centre, facing the second top gent.

(8 bars)

(h) Top lady and the two top gents now weave through a figure-eight movement. The lady passes the second gent right shoulder to right as she turns clockwise into his position, then passes her own partner right shoulder to right and the second gent left shoulder to left as she dances back across the set. She passes her own partner left shoulder to left as she turns anticlockwise into her own place. The two gents pass left shoulder to left the first time they meet and right shoulder to right the second time. (Top lady passes right right left left, second gent passes right left left right and top gent passes left right right left.) (8 bars)

(i) Top couples swing in place in waltz hold. (8 bars)

(j) Repeat (e) to (i) with first side lady (on the left) leading. (40 bars)

(j) Repeat (e) to (i) with second top lady leading. (40 bars)

(k) Repeat (e) to (i) with second side lady (on the right) leading. (40 bars)

(l) All repeat (a) to (d). (40 bars)

FIGURE 2: JIG (192 BARS)

(a) All couples dance the square ('luascadh'). In waltz hold, with the gents' backs to the centre, they slide to the position on their right, dancing 1 2 3 hop, lifting their second foot (the gent's right and the lady's left) as they hop on the first one. They now dance 1 hop (on the second foot as they lift the first one) and 1 hop (on the first foot as they lift the second one) as they turn slightly clockwise so that the ladies' backs are to the centre. From here they repeat the movement to the next position, all starting on their second foot (the gent's right and the lady's left) this time. (8 bars)

(b) Repeat (a), dancing back to place. (8 bars)

(c) All slide to the centre and house to the opposite positions. (8 bars)

(d) All slide to the centre and house back to home positions. (8 bars)

(e) All couples house around. (8 bars)

(f) All turn from their partners to face the person in the corner. All dance steps (down, up, 1 2 3) on both feet, then swing in *céilí* hold. (8 bars)

(g) Dancing from the swing into a circle with ladies facing out and gents facing in, all lead around to the right, with each gent holding his partner's hand over her shoulder and the other lady's hand behind him, as in the Ballycommon Set. (8 bars)

(h) Reforming the circle with ladies facing out and gents facing in, all dance steps (8 bars), then swing (8 bars). (16 bars)

(i) Repeat (a) to (h). (72 bars)

(j) All repeat (a) to (e). (40 bars)

FIGURE 3: POLKA (120 BARS)

(a) All advance and retire twice in a circle. (8 bars)

(b) All couples swing in waltz hold. (8 bars)

(c) All dance the polka (Borlin, without the jump) and house. (24 bars)

(d) Holding crossed hands, all couples square to the left, reverse to opposite positions, square left again and reverse back to home.   (8 bars)

(e) Top couples advance and retire, then cross anticlockwise to face in at the opposite side. Side couples repeat, starting two bars behind top couples.   (8 bars)

(f) All couples dance (e) again, crossing back to place.   (8 bars)

(g) All couples square again.   (8 bars)

(h) All couples dance (a) to (c) again.   (40 bars)

FIGURE 4: HORNPIPE (112 BARS)

(a) In waltz hold, starting in the gent's corner, all couples dance 'sevens' in a square around the set, to finish back at home.   (8 bars)

(b) All couples house around.   (8 bars)

(c) Top gents dance to the centre and double, hooking left arms, then dance forward, right shoulder to right with the opposite lady, and hook right arms to turn around her into the opposite gent's position.   (8 bars)

(d) Side gents repeat (c).   (8 bars)

(e) Top couples 'gallop' across, dancing 'sevens', side couples follow, then all repeat back to where they started in the opposite positions.   (8 bars)

(f) All couples house around.   (8 bars)

(g) Repeat (a) to (f).   (48 bars)

(h) All dance (a) and (b) again, doubling the last two bars.   (8 bars)

Slip and Slide Polka Set

This set, from County Monaghan, was given to me by dancing teacher Anna Pegley of Leixlip, County Kildare.

Figure 1: Polka (128 bars)

(a) Body: Taking waltz hold, all couples dance four 'threes' to the position on the right, ladies reversing and gents dancing forward (4 bars), then dance into opposite positions, turning twice (4 bars).

(8 bars)

(b) All repeat (a), starting in opposite positions and dancing back to home. (8 bars)

(c) All couples house around. (8 bars)

(d) All couples swing in waltz hold. (8 bars)

(e) Top ladies dance the long chain. They chain with right hands in the centre, left (low) around opposite gent, right in the centre again and left around their own partners into place (8 bars). They then chain with right hands in the centre again, turning twice, left around the opposite gent, and dance back to home, passing right shoulder to right. (8 bars). (16 bars)

(f) Top couples house around each other. (8 bars)

(g) 'Slip and slide': All couples slide to the position on the right and turn slightly, dancing (1 2, 1 2 3), then reverse to the next position, starting on the other foot, and repeat the moves as they dance around the set to home. (8 bars)

(h) All couples house around. (8 bars)

(i) Side couples dance (e) and (f). (24 bars)

(j) All couples dance (g) and (h) again, then swing. (24 bars)

Figure 2: Polka (176 bars)

(a) All couples dance the body, as in Figure 1 (a) and (b). (16 bars)

(b) All couples house around. (8 bars)

(c) All couples swing in waltz hold. (8 bars)

(d) First top couple house inside. (8 bars)

(e) First top couple dance the 'slip and slide' inside: slide to the right and turn, dancing (1 2, 1 2 3), reverse to the next position and turn, then repeat the movements back to place. (8 bars)

(f) All couples dance the 'slip and slide' around the house. (8 bars)

(g) All couples house around. (8 bars)

(h) Repeat (d) to (g) three times, with first side couple (on the left), second top couple and second side couple leading in turn. (96 bars)

(i) All couples swing. (8 bars)

FIGURE 3: JIG (192 BARS)

(a) All couples swing. (8 bars)

(b) All couples house around. (8 bars)

(c) Top couples slide towards each other in the centre (2 bars), slide through the opposite couple, ladies reversing from their partners to pass between the other couple (2 bars), slide forward again towards the next (opposite) position (2 bars) and turn clockwise into the opposite position (2 bars). (8 bars)

(d) Top couples repeat (c), sliding back to turn into their own places.(8 bars)

(e) Top couples house around each other. (8 bars)

(f) All couples dance the 'slip and slide' around the house. (8 bars)

(g) All couples house around. (8 bars)

(h) Repeat (c) to (g) with side couples dancing (c), (d) and (e). (40 bars)

(i) Repeat (c) to (h). (80 bars)

(j) All couples swing. (8 bars)

FIGURE 4: HORNPIPE (120 BARS)

(a) Body: All couples dance one step to the centre and back, turn clockwise to the position on the right (4 bars), then repeat the movements three times, dancing around the set. (16 bars)

(b) Top couples face the side couple on their right. All advance (hop 1 2 3, hop 1 2 3) and retire (hop 1 2 3, hop 1 2 3), then each top lady and opposite side lady change places, passing left shoulder to left and turning anticlockwise under the opposite gent's right arm into place beside him. (8 bars)

(c) Top couples face left and side couples face right. All couples advance and retire once, then ladies change places, as in (b). (8 bars)

(d) Repeat (b) and (c). Ladies change partners twice more to get around to their own places. Top ladies move to the right each time and side ladies move to the left. (16 bars)

(e) All couples dance the body again. (16 bars)

(f) Top couples face the side couple on their left. All advance and retire once, then top gents change places with the opposite side gent, passing right shoulder to right, all gents taking the new lady's right hand. The lady turns anticlockwise under the gent's arm as he dances into place. Top gents dance outside the lady as she turns, while side gents dance into place facing her. (8 bars)

(g) Top couples face the side couple on their right this time. All couples advance and retire, then the gents change places, as in (f). (8 bars)

(h) Repeat (f) and (g). Gents change partners twice more as they move around the set to their own places. Top gents move left and side gents move right each time. (16 bars)

(i) All couples dance the body again. (16 bars)

SNEEM SET

This south Kerry set has been popularised by dancing teacher Timmy MacCarthy.

FIGURE 1: POLKA (144 BARS)

(a) All four couples dance the polka: dance in and back, turn clockwise to the next position on the right and repeat the movements three times, going around the set to home. (16 bars)

(b) All couples dance around the house. (8 bars)

(c) Top couples join right hands in the centre and dance one clockwise turn around the centre to home. (8 bars)

(d) Top couples swing in waltz hold. (8 bars)

(e) Top ladies chain in the centre, turn arm to arm around opposite gent and dance back to home. (8 bars)

(f) Top couples house around each other. (8 bars)

(g) All couples dance the polka and house again. (24 bars)

(h) All repeat (c) to (g), with side couples dancing (c) to (f). (56 bars)

FIGURE 2: POLKA (112 BARS)

(a) All four couples dance the polka: dance in and back, turn clockwise to the next position on the right and repeat the movements three times, going around the set to home. (16 bars)

(b) All couples dance around the house. (8 bars)

(c) Top couples slide to the centre and back, then dance one turn in place. (8 bars)

(d) Top couples repeat (c). (8 bars)

(e) All couples dance the polka and house again. (24 bars)

(f) Repeat (c) to (e) with side couples dancing (c) and (d). (40 bars)

FIGURE 3: POLKA (112 BARS)

(a) All four couples dance the polka: dance in and back, turn clockwise to the next position on the right and repeat the movements three times, going around the set to home. (16 bars)

(b) All couples dance around the house. (8 bars)

(c) The four ladies join right hands in the centre, dance across the set and turn with left arm around the opposite gents, then chain back to home. (8 bars)

(d) All couples swing in place. (8 bars)

(e) In waltz hold, all couples dance four steps, stepping in and back twice, then turn twice, moving to opposite positions. (8 bars)

(f) Repeat (e), crossing back to home. (8 bars)

(g) All couples dance around the house. (8 bars)

(h) All repeat (c) to (g). (40 bars)

FIGURE 4: POLKA (96 BARS)

(a) All four couples dance the polka: dance in and back, turn clockwise to the next position on the right and repeat the movements three times, going around the set to home. (16 bars)

(b) All couples dance around the house. (8 bars)

(c) Holding hands in a circle, all dancers advance and retire once, then dance clockwise in the circle to opposite positions. (8 bars)

(d) Holding hands in a circle, all dancers advance and retire once, then dance clockwise in the circle back to home. (8 bars)

(e) All lead around anticlockwise, each gent's arm around his partner's waist and her hand on his shoulder. (8 bars)

(f) All couples house around. (8 bars)

(g) All repeat (c) to (f). (32 bars)

FIGURE 5: SLIDE (168 BARS)

(a) All four couples dance the polka: dance in and back, turn clockwise to the next position on the right and repeat the movements three times, going around the set to home. (16 bars)

(b) All couples dance around the house. (8 bars)

(c) Top couples slide to the centre and back, then house to opposite positions. (8 bars)

(d) Top couples slide to the centre and back, then house to home. (8 bars)

(e) Top couples slide to the centre and back, then top ladies cross right shoulder to right to opposite lady's positions. (8 bars)

(f) Top couples house with new partners. (8 bars)

(g) Top couples slide to the centre and back with new partners (4 bars), then ladies cross, taking their own partner's left hand and turning around him into their own position (4 bars). They now continue the chain movement, taking the other lady's hand in the centre, turning with their left hand around the opposite gent and chaining back to place (8 bars). (16 bars)

(h) Top couples house again. (8 bars)

(i) Side couples dance (c) to (h). (56 bars)

(j) All four couples dance the polka: dance in and back, turn clockwise to the next position on the right and repeat the movements three times, going around the set to home.   (16 bars)

(k) All couples dance around the house.   (8 bars)

FIGURE 6: HORNPIPE (160 BARS)

(a) All four couples dance the body using the hornpipe steps: dance in and back, turn clockwise to the next position on the right and repeat the movements three times, going around the set to home.

    (16 bars)

(b) All couples dance around the house.   (8 bars)

(c) Holding hands in a circle, all dancers step in and back three times (6 bars), then the gents step in and back again while the ladies move outside them to the next lady's position on the right (2 bars).

    (8 bars)

(d) All repeat the body and house with new partners.   (24 bars)

(e) Repeat (c) and (d) three times, so that all dance the last body and house with their own partners.   (96 bars)

SOURIS SET

(PRINCE EDWARD ISLAND)

This set was sent to me by Elizabeth MacDonald, who teaches set dancing in the Maritime Provinces of Canada, particularly in Halifax, Nova Scotia, where she lives. Elizabeth learned about the set, which is one of a number danced on the island, from Helen Conboy and the Prince Edward Island set dancers. In 1998 I had the privilege of visiting Nova Scotia and Prince Edward Island, where I spent a lovely evening dancing with Helen, her husband Gary and friends of theirs. Elizabeth has been collecting square sets in the Maritimes for a number of years and will be publishing a collection of them. The set is described here as it is danced in Goose River, Prince Edward Island. It traditionally featured four or six couples but now seems to be danced with any number of couples. The set is danced with a smooth, 'slide-y' style of walk and a 'hug' hold, similar to that used in the Connemara Jig Set. It is danced to jigs and reels; on Prince Edward Island, the choice of rhythm for each figure is left to the musicians. I have slightly adapted Elizabeth's instructions to give a description of how the set can be danced by four couples. All numbers of bars given are approximate and apply to the four- or six-couple version of the set.

FIGURE 1 (136 BARS): CIRCLE, EVERYONE HOLDING HANDS

(a) Circle left: All couples join hands and go once around clockwise until back in original positions. (8 bars)

(b) Swing: All swing in the 'hug' hold. (8 bars)

(c) Promenade: Anticlockwise, gent with right arm around partner's waist, lady's left hand on gent's right shoulder. (8 bars)

(d) Tops and sides: Arch – top couples continue to face anticlockwise around the set while side couples turn on the spot to face them. Join hands and circle halfway around to the opposite position. (4 bars) The couples go back home as follows: the top couple make an arch and advance towards the side couple. The side lady goes under the arch while her partner passes on outside to meet her in the opposite position. The gent and lady of each couple then pass left shoulder to left. Finish with top and side couples still facing each other. (4 bars) (8 bars)

(e) Chain and swing: Top ladies and side ladies chain across by giving right hands (2 bars), and then swing with the opposite man (6 bars). Ladies chain back (2 bars) and swing with partner (6 bars). (16 bars)

[*Variation*: Circle all the way around (8 bars) and ladies chain as in (e).(16 bars)]

(g) Promenade as in (c). (8 bars)
(h) Repeat (d) and (e) with top couples turning to face side couples – all face the couple on the other side. (24 bars)
(i) Promenade as in (c). (8 bars)
(j) Grand chain (referred to locally as 'grand change all'): Twice around the circle, beginning by giving right hand to partner. (32 bars)

[*Note*: In Maritime Canada, chains are often danced with the men turning the ladies under the arm as they pass by – anticlockwise under the right arm and clockwise under the left.]

(k) Promenade as in (c) around the circle to finish. (8 bars)

FIGURE 2 (80 BARS): CIRCLE, ALL HOLDING HANDS
(a) Advance and retire and swing: Advance and retire once (4 bars) and swing (4 bars) (8 bars)

[*Variation 1*: Advance and retire (4 bars), then swing (12 bars) (16 bars)
Variation 2: No advance and retire. Swing (8 bars) (8 bars)]

(b) Promenade anticlockwise, man's right arm around partner's waist, lady's left hand on man's right shoulder. (8 bars)
(c) Each lady moves on to the man directly ahead of her. He turns back to meet her and swings. (8 bars)
(d) Repeat (b) and (c) until back with original partner for the final swing. (48 bars)

FIGURE 3 (112 BARS): TWO CIRCLES; LADIES JOINING HANDS ON THE INSIDE, MEN JOINING HANDS ON THE OUTSIDE
(a) Concentric circles and interlace: Ladies stand or step-dance on the spot while men dance clockwise around them, stopping when they arrive back at their original position on the left of their partners.

(6 bars) Interlace: Still holding hands, ladies move back while men raise their joined hands up and over the ladies' heads. Each gent's right hand comes up and over his partner's head while his left hand comes up and over the head of the lady on his left. (2 bars). (8 bars)

(b) All advance and retire twice. In local terminology, the advance-and-retire movement is called the 'surge'. (8 bars)

(c) All couples swing. (8 bars)

(d) Promenade anticlockwise, man's right arm around partner's waist, lady's left hand on man's right shoulder. (8 bars)

(e) Concentric circles and interlace: Gents stand or step-dance on the spot while ladies dance clockwise around them, stopping when they arrive back at their original position on the right of their partners. (6 bars) Still holding hands, gents move back while ladies raise their joined hands up and over the gents' heads. Each lady's left hand comes up and over his partner's head while her right hand comes up and over the head of the gent on her right. (2 bars). (8 bars)

(f) All repeat (b) to (d). (24 bars)

(g) Grand chain: Twice around the circle, beginning by giving right hand to partner. (32 bars)

(h) Promenade around the circle and off the floor, each gent accompanying his partner back to her seat. (8 bars)

[*Note*: Sometimes the promenade after the swing is omitted and danced only at the end of the figure.]

STEP-DANCE: When the reel rhythm is played, dancers may substitute step-dance footwork for the walk. This option can be used when dancing on the spot (Figure 3) or while doing the chain or promenade, or both. The variation used frequently on Prince Edward Island is as follows:

Hop left foot (count '1'), shuffle right foot (count 'and 2'), hop left foot, touch right foot to floor (count 'and 3'), hop left foot (count '4'), shuffle right foot (count 'and a'). Repeat on opposite side ('5, and 6, and 7, 8 and a'). In an eight-bar phrase, this pattern is repeated four times.

TORY ISLAND SET

This set was collected from local dancers on Tory Island, County Donegal, by dancing master Connie Ryan. It was first published by Eileen O'Doherty in her set-dancing book The Walking Polka. My thanks to Eileen and to Betty McCoy for their help in teaching me the set. All swings in this set are 'hug' swings – dancers have their right arm around their partner's waist and their left hand holding the top part of their partner's arm.

FIGURE 1: SLIDE (88 BARS)

(a) All circle, advance and retire twice. (8 bars)

(b) All couples swing: this is the 'hug' swing, as in the Tory Lancers, all with their right arm around their partner's waist and their left hand holding the top part of their partner's arm. (8 bars)

(c) Top couples dance clockwise in single file around the inside of the set. To begin the movement, each lady dances to her left, passing in front of her partner, and each gent follows his partner. During the last two bars, each lady turns clockwise to face her partner as he finishes facing her from her position. (8 bars)

(d) Top couples swing in the 'hug' swing. (8 bars)

(e) Top couples repeat (c) and (d). (16 bars)

(f) Side couples dance (c) to (e) with top couples swinging at (d) the last time. (32 bars)

FIGURE 2: POLKA (120 BARS)

(a) All circle, advance and retire twice. (8 bars)

(b) All couples swing the hug swing. (8 bars)

(c) Holding right hand in right, top couples advance and retire once, then dance clockwise to opposite positions, facing their partners all the time. (8 bars)

(d) Top couples repeat (c), dancing back to their own places. During the last two bars, each lady reverses into her partner's position while the gents follow them, dancing into the ladies' positions. (8 bars)

(e) Top couples swing. Each dancer starts the swing in their partner's position and finishes in their own. (8 bars)

(f) Top couples repeat (c) to (e). (24 bars)

(g) Side couples dance (c) to (f), top couples swinging also the last time at (f). (48 bars)

FIGURE 3: POLKA (152 BARS)

(a) All circle, advance and retire twice.   (8 bars)

(b) All couples swing the hug swing.   (8 bars)

(c) Top ladies chain with right hands in the centre, take left hand in left with the opposite gent and dance anticlockwise around him, turning clockwise under his arm. The gent stays facing into the set, dancing forward to the right as the lady is dancing around him, then reverses back into his own position as she starts to cross back home. Ladies pass right shoulder to right in the centre on the way back and turn clockwise into their own places.   (8 bars)

(d) Top couples swing the hug swing.   (8 bars)

(e) Top gent and opposite lady dance in and swing in the centre, each of them finishing the swing with their back to the couple on the right of their original home position.   (8 bars)

(f) Top gent takes his partner's right hand in his left and takes her anticlockwise across to the opposite position, the lady turning clockwise into the opposite lady's place, taking the gent's right hand in her left as she does so and letting his left hand go. At the same time, second top lady takes her partner's right hand in her left and leads him across to the first top position (2 bars). Both couples now advance and retire once (4 bars), then ladies move forward to the left, facing their partners, and cross clockwise, the ladies reversing into their partners' positions while the gents face them from the ladies' positions (2 bars).   (8 bars)

(g) Top couples swing in the hug swing.   (8 bars)

(h) Top couples repeat (e) to (g) with top lady and second gent leading.   (24 bars)

(i) Side couples dance (c) to (h). The first side couple are on the left of the first top couple. Top couples also swing at (g) the last time.   (64 bars)

FIGURE 4: POLKA (216 BARS)

(a) All circle, advance and retire twice.   (8 bars)

(b) All couples swing in the hug swing.   (8 bars)

(c) Top ladies chain with right hands in the centre, take left hand in left with the opposite gent and dance anticlockwise around him, turning clockwise under his arm. The gent stays facing into the set, dancing forward to the right as the lady is dancing around him, then reverses back into his own position as she starts to cross back home. Ladies pass right shoulder to right in the centre on the way back and turn clockwise into their own places.   (8 bars)

(d) Top couples swing in the hug swing. (8 bars)

(e) Each top gent places his right arm around his partner's waist while she places her left arm on his right shoulder. Both couples advance to the centre and the second lady turns anticlockwise to stand in beside the top gent, then both gents retire, ladies going with the first top gent (4 bars). All four advance and retire again, both ladies still with the first top gent (4 bars). (8 bars)

(f) All four advance to the centre again and both ladies join the second top gent, the first lady turning anticlockwise and the second lady turning clockwise to place their hands on his shoulders, then both gents retire, ladies going with the second gent this time (4 bars). All advance and retire again, ladies still with the second top gent. (8 bars)

(g) First top lady dances clockwise across and turns anticlockwise into her partner's position, followed by the second top gent, who faces her from her position. At the same time, the top gent crosses clockwise to the opposite lady's position while she dances into her own partner's position, turning anticlockwise to face him, and all swing opposite partners. (8 bars)

(h) Top ladies chain with right hands in the centre, take left hand in left with their own partner and dance anticlockwise around him, turning clockwise under his arm as they dance into the opposite lady's position. The gent stays facing into the set, dancing forward to the right as the lady is dancing around him, and reversing back into place beside her (4 bars). The top ladies cross right shoulder to right and turn anticlockwise into their partners' positions, then the top gents cross clockwise into their own partners' positions (4 bars). (8 bars)

(i) Top couples swing, all finishing in their own positions. (8 bars)

(j) Top couples repeat (e) to (i) with second top couple leading. (40 bars)

(k) Side couples dance (c) to (j) with each side couple leading in turn. Top couples also swing at (i) the last time. (96 bars)

FIGURE 5: SLIDE (136 BARS)

(a) All circle, advance and retire twice. (8 bars)

(b) All couples swing in the 'hug' swing. (8 bars)

(c) All couples take crossed hands behind their backs. Top couples advance and, as they retire, side couples advance. Then as side couples retire, top couples advance again, and as they retire this time side couples advance again. (8 bars)

(d) As side couples retire for the second time and dance on the spot, top couples advance to their right to face the side couple there and reverse into opposite positions (4 bars). As they dance on the spot in opposite positions, side couples advance to their right and reverse into their opposite positions (4 bars). (8 bars)

(e) All couples repeat (c) and (d), to finish back in their own positions. (16 bars)

(f) Top ladies chain with right hands in the centre, take left hand in left with the opposite gent and dance anticlockwise around him, turning clockwise under his arm. The gent stays facing into the set, dancing forward to the right as the lady is dancing around him, then he reverses back into his own position as she starts to cross back home. Ladies pass right shoulder to right in the centre on the way back and turn clockwise into their own places. (8 bars)

(g) Top couples swing in the hug swing. (8 bars)

(h) Repeat (c) to (g) with side couples leading. (48 bars)

(i) All circle, advance and retire twice. (8 bars)

(j) All couples swing in the hug swing. (8 bars)

TOURNAFULLA SET

This set was given to me by Miley Costello of Limerick during the
Ballyshannon Set Dancing Weekend in 1999.

FIGURE 1: SLIDE (192 BARS)

(a) All dance the body, as in the Sliabh Luachra.　　　　　　(16 bars)

(b) Top couples slide to the centre and back, then dance one turn in
place.　　　　　　(8 bars)

(c) Top ladies chain with right hands in the centre, turn opposite gent
twice with left hand, chain with right hands in the centre again and
dance back home.　　　　　　(8 bars)

(d) Top couples swing (wheel) in waltz hold.　　　　　　(8 bars)

(e) All dance the body, as in the Sliabh Luachra.　　　　　　(16 bars)

(f) Side couples dance (b) to (d).　　　　　　(24 bars)

(g) All dance the body, as in the Sliabh Luachra.　　　　　　(16 bars)

(h) All repeat (b) to (g).　　　　　　(80 bars)

(i) All couples house around.　　　　　　(8 bars)

FIGURE 2: SLIDE (160 BARS)

(a) All dance the body, as in the Sliabh Luachra.　　　　　　(16 bars)

(b) First top couple house inside.　　　　　　(8 bars)

(c) First top couple slide (gallop) to the centre and back, then swing.
　　　　　　(8 bars)

(d) All dance the body, as in the Sliabh Luachra.　　　　　　(16 bars)

(e) Repeat (b), (c) and (d) with side couple on the left, opposite top
couple and side couple on the right leading in turn.　　　　　　(96 bars)

(f) All couples house around.　　　　　　(8 bars)

FIGURE 3: SLIDE (192 BARS)

(a) All dance the body, as in the Sliabh Luachra.　　　　　　(16 bars)

(b) Top couples slide to the centre and back holding right hands, then
ladies change places, passing right shoulder to right, and gents
change, passing left shoulder to left.　　　　　　(8 bars)

(c) Top couples slide to the centre and back holding right hands, then
ladies change places, passing right shoulder to right, and gents
change, passing left shoulder to left, all moving in to form a circle
of four in the centre with arms around the waist.　　　　　　(8 bars)

(d) Top couples swing in four in the centre (6 bars) and swing their partners back to place, dancing one full turn (2 bars).   (8 bars)

(e) All dance the body, as in the Sliabh Luachra.   (16 bars)

(f) Side couples dance (b) to (d).   (24 bars)

(g) All dance the body, as in the Sliabh Luachra.   (16 bars)

(h) All repeat (b) to (g).   (80 bars)

(i) All house around.   (8 bars)

FIGURE 4: POLKAS (88 BARS)

(a) All couples take waltz hold and dance anticlockwise around the set, ladies reversing and gents dancing forward all the way round.   (8 bars)

(b) All dance a 'diamond' square, dancing a gallop step to each position.   (8 bars)

(c) The four ladies join right hands in the centre, dance across and turn twice with left arms around the opposite gent, then join right hands in the centre again, dance back to place and swing their partners.   (16 bars)

(d) All repeat (a) to (c).   (32 bars)

(e) All repeat (a) and (b).   (16 bars)

FIGURE 5: HORNPIPE (128 BARS)

(a) All couples dance the body, with hornpipe steps: they dance in (hop 1 2 3), gents hopping on their right foot, ladies on their left foot, then dance back (stamp 1 2 3), gents stamping on their right foot and dancing the first step out on the right foot also, ladies on their left foot (2 bars). Now all couples turn clockwise to the position on their right (hop 1 2 3, hop 1 2 3) (2 bars). They repeat all movements three times to get back home.   (16 bars)

(b) All couples house around.   (8 bars)

(c) The four gents dance in and back as in (a), while the ladies dance on to join the gent on the right (2 bars), then all, with new partners, turn clockwise to the position on their right (2 bars). All couples now dance the body movements in (a), going around to the gents' original positions (12 bars).   (16 bars)

(d) All couples dance around the house.   (8 bars)

(e) Repeat (c) and (d), ladies now dancing with the opposite gent.   (24 bars)

(f) Repeat (c) and (d), ladies dancing with the gent to the left of their own positions.   (24 bars)

(g) Repeat (c) and (d) again, ladies now back dancing with their own partners.   (24 bars)

TRURO WALTZ QUADRILLES

I learned this beautiful dance at a Senior Citizens' Club dance in Truro, Nova Scotia, during Easter 1999. My trip there and our participation in the evening's dancing was arranged by Elizabeth MacDonald, a dancing teacher, from Halifax, Nova Scotia. My thanks to the dancers in Truro for their welcome and hospitality and to Elizabeth for arranging the trip and for her guidance in recording the dance. The numbers of bars of music given are approximate as some of the movements can take longer at times.

FIGURE 1: WALTZ

(a) Top ladies waltz across, dancing forward and then turning into the opposite position. (2 bars)

(b) Top gents waltz across, dancing forward and then turning into the opposite position. (2 bars)

(c) Top couples dance at home in opposite positions. (8 bars)

(d) Top couples repeat (a) and (b), dancing back to home. (4 bars)

(e) All couples dance around the house slowly. (32 bars)

(f) Repeat (a) to (e) with side couples dancing (a) to (d). (48 bars)

FIGURE 2: WALTZ

(a) Taking their partner's right hand in their right, all dancers step forward and back, then pass their partners by, with each lady turning under the gent's right hand (4 bars). Then all give their left hands to the next person they meet and repeat the movements, each lady turning under the gent's left hand (4 bars). The movements are repeated with the next two people as all chain to opposite positions (8 bars). (16 bars)

(b) All couples waltz back to home with their own partners. (16 bars)

(c) Repeat (a) and (b) three more times. (96 bars)

FIGURE 3: WALTZ

(a) Starting in a circle, all step forward and back once (2 bars), then each gent takes the lady on his left in waltz hold and they waltz in his place, turning three times (6 bars). (8 bars)

(b) All waltz around the house with their new partners and let each other go at the end, ladies finishing in the lady's position to the right of their own. (16 bars)

(c) Repeat (a) and (b) three times, ladies moving on at (a) each time
to dance with the next gent. They finish with their own partners
when they move on the last time. (72 bars)

FIGURE 4: WALTZ

(a) All gents turn to their left and ladies turn to their right. Each gent
takes the corner lady's right hand in his left and they step forward
towards each other and back, taking waltz hold (2 bars), then
waltz in the corner and finish by dancing back to take their own
partners in waltz hold during the last few bars. (16 bars)
(b) All waltz around the house with their own partners. (16 bars)
(c) Repeat (a) and (b) three times. (96 bars)
(d) All chain all round, with the ladies turning under each gent's hand
– right hand the first time, left hand the second – and continue
until back home. (32 bars)
(e) All break away into a general waltz around the hall.

TYRAWLEY SET

This traditional set from the barony of Tyrawley in north County Mayo was taught by Martin Bolger at the Galway Set Dancing Weekend in 1997.

FIGURE 1: JIG (264 BARS)

(a) Top couples square (face on): Dance to face the couple on their left, reverse into the positions opposite their own, dance to face the couple on their left from there and reverse to home positions.

(8 bars)

(b) Top couples swing in *céilí* hold, holding right hands at shoulder height and holding their partner's right elbow with their left hand.

(8 bars)

(c) Top ladies chain with right arms in the centre, left arm to opposite gent and right arm in the centre as they dance back to place. (8 bars)

(d) Top couples square again, as at (a). (8 bars)

(e) Side couples dance (a) to (d). (32 bars)

(f) All ladies dance to the left, passing in front of their partners. Gents turn left to follow them as they dance clockwise around the set to home. As they reach home, each lady turns clockwise to take her partner's right hand again. (8 bars)

(g) All couples swing, starting from their own partner's position. (8 bars)

(h) All repeat (f) and (g). (16 bars)

(i) Top gent and opposite lady swing in the centre (6 bars) and reverse to place. (8 bars)

(j) Top couples square again, as in (a). (8 bars)

(k) Top couples chain. (8 bars)

(l) Top couples house around each other in waltz hold. (8 bars)

(m) Top couples swing in four in the centre ('bundle of fun'), breaking back to place during the last two bars. (8 bars)

(n) Repeat (i) to (m) with top lady and second top gent swinging at (i). (40 bars)

(o) Side couples dance (i) to (n). First side couple are on the left. (80 bars)

FIGURE 2: POLKA (136 BARS)

(a) Top couples dance 'sevens' across the set, gents passing back to back. Starting by stepping onto their leading foot and keeping most of their weight on it as they cross, they dance fourteen steps on the way over. Changing weight to lead on the other foot, they dance sevens back to place, ladies passing back to back this time.

| | (8 bars) |

(b) Top couples house around each other. (8 bars)

(c) Top ladies chain, as in Figure 1(c). (8 bars)

(d) Top couples swing while side couples dance in and back four times in waltz hold. (8 bars)

(e) Top couples repeat (a) to (d). (32 bars)

(e) Side couples dance (a) to (e). (64 bars)

FIGURE 3: REEL (104 BARS)

(a) Holding hands in a circle, all advance and retire twice. (8 bars)

(b) All ladies swing the gent on their right, as in Figure 1. (8 bars)

(c) Each gent places his right arm around his new partner's waist and all lead around. (8 bars)

(d) All repeat (a) to (c) until leading around with their own partners. (72 bars)

VICTORIA JIG SET

This version of the Victoria Set was taught by the late Jer McAuliffe of Newmarket, County Cork. Jer also taught a version of the set danced with six couples.

FIGURE 1: JIG (192 BARS)

(a) All couples dance around the house in waltz hold, ladies reversing to each position and gents dancing forward. They turn slightly anticlockwise in each position. This movement is called shunting.
(8 bars)

(b) All couples house around, turning clockwise four times. (8 bars)

(c) First top couple 'show the lady' (house inside). (8 bars)

(d) First top couple face the couple on their left (first side couple), both couples taking their partner's right hand in their right. They advance (1 2, 1 2 3) and retire (1 2, 1 2 3) twice. (8 bars)

(e) Top couples house around each other. (8 bars)

(f) All gents swing the lady on their left, then swing their partners. (16 bars)

(g) Repeat (c) to (f) with first side couple (on the left), second top couple and second side couple leading in turn. (120 bars)

(h) All couples square around the house , dancing (1 2, 1 2 3) four times. They dance forward to the first position on the right, reverse, starting on the other foot, to the next position and repeat the movements back to home. (8 bars)

FIGURE 2: JIG (224 BARS)

(a) All couples dance around the house, dancing the shunting movement (8 bars), then house around (8 bars). (16 bars)

(b) First top couple 'show the lady'. (8 bars)

(c) First top couple face the couple on their left. Both couples advance and retire once, then ladies cross, passing right shoulder to right, and gents cross, passing left shoulder to left. (8 bars)

(d) Repeat (c), both couples crossing back to place. (8 bars)

(e) Top couples house around each other. (8 bars)

(f) All gents swing the lady on the left, then swing their partners. (16 bars)

(g) Repeat (b) to (f) with first side couple, second top couple and second side couple leading in turn. (144 bars)

(h) All couples square around the house. (8 bars)

FIGURE 3: JIG (280 BARS

(a) All couples dance around the house, dancing the shunting movement (8 bars), then house around. (8 bars)

(b) First top couple 'show the lady'. (8 bars)

(c) Top couples advance and retire, right hand in right (4 bars). They advance again and, as their partners retire, top lady and second top gent change places, passing right shoulder to right (4 bars). The two gents are now in the top position and the two ladies are in the second top position, facing them. (8 bars)

(d) Top gents and ladies advance and retire (no hands) (4 bars). They advance again, and as second top lady and gent retire (second gent to top position, second lady to her own position), top gent and top lady cross over, passing right shoulder to right (4 bars). (8 bars)

(e) Each top gent swings the opposite lady in her position. (8 bars)

(f) Top gents cross, right shoulder to right, and swing their own partners. (8 bars)

(g) Top couples house around each other. (8 bars)

(h) All gents swing the lady on their left, then swing their partners. (16 bars)

(i) Repeat (b) to (h) with first side couple, second top couple and second side couple leading in turn. (192 bars)

(j) All couples square around the house. (8 bars)

FIGURE 4: JIG (288 BARS)

(a) All couples dance around the house, dancing the shunting movement (8 bars), then house around (8 bars). (16 bars)

(b) First top couple 'show the lady'. (8 bars)

(c) Starting with the lady on his left (first side lady) and finishing with his own partner, top gent swings with each lady in turn. (32 bars)

(d) Top couples house around each other. (8 bars)

(e) All gents swing the lady on their left, then swing their partners. (16 bars)

(f) Repeat (b) to (e) with first side couple, second top couple and second side couple leading in turn. (192 bars)

(g) All couples square around the house. (8 bars)

FIGURE 5 : REEL (272 BARS)

(a) All couples lead around, holding crossed hands in front. (8 bars)

(b) With their backs to the centre, the gents turn the ladies, left hand in left, four times (8 bars), then all couples swing (8 bars). (16 bars)

(c) Top couples square anticlockwise all round the centre, dancing 'sevens' along each side of the square. (8 bars)

(d) Top couples house around each other. (8 bars)

(e) Top gents cross (2 bars) and swing the opposite lady (6 bars). (8 bars)

(f) Top gents link left arms in the centre and dance around each other (6 bars), then double around each other (2 bars), breaking away to their own partners from the double. (8 bars)

(g) Repeat (a) to (f) with side couples leading. (56 bars)

(h) Repeat (a) to (g), with all couples dancing again. (112 bars)

(i) All dance (a) and (b) again. (24 bars)

(j) All couples dance the 'diamond' square – they dance sevens all around the house. (8 bars)

(k) All couples house around. (8 bars)

West Limerick Polka Set

*This version of the set was danced by Tim Murphy, Gerry O'Sullivan
and their set during a session at the Tralee Shindig Workshop
in January 1997.*

Figure 1 : Polka (160 bars)

(a) All four couples dance the body: dance in and back, turn
clockwise to the next position on the right and repeat the
movements three times, going around the set to home. (16 bars)

(b) Top ladies chain with right hands in the centre, take left hands
with opposite gent to turn anticlockwise twice under his arm, as
gents turn anticlockwise, then chain back to place. (8 bars)

(c) Top couples swing in place in waltz hold. (8 bars)

(d) All dance the body again. (16 bars)

(e) Side couples dance the ladies' chain and swing. (16 bars)

(f) All dance the body again. (16 bars)

(g) Repeat (b) to (f). (64 bars)

(h) All couples house around. (8 bars)

Figure 2 : Polka (160 bars)

(a) All couples dance the body, as in Figure 1. (16 bars)

(b) First top couple house inside ('show the lady') (8 bars), then all
couples slide to the centre with arms around each other in a circle
and slide back; the leading couple turn once in place (8 bars). (16 bars)

(c) All couples dance the body again. (16 bars)

(d) First side couple (on the left) dance (b). (16 bars)

(e) All couples dance the body. (16 bars)

(f) Second top couple dance (b). (16 bars)

(g) All couples dance the body. (16 bars)

(h) Second side couple dance (b). (16 bars)

(i) All couples dance the body, then house around. (24 bars)

Figure 3 : Slide (192 bars)

(a) All couples dance the body. (16 bars)

(b) Top couples take right hands, advance to the centre and back.
Then, as the opposite lady passes her right shoulder to right, going
to the top lady's position, the top gent turns the top lady clockwise
to his left-hand side, to a position slightly in front of him, and the

179

opposite gent passes under their arch on his way to the top gent's position, while the top couple cross to face in from the opposite top position. (8 bars)

(c) Top couples repeat (b), dancing back to place, then swing. (16 bars)

(d) All couples dance the body again. (16 bars)

(e) Side couples dance (b) and (c), first side couple making the arch.

(24 bars)

(f) All couples dance the body again. (16 bars)

(g) Repeat (b) to (f) with second couples leading. (80 bars)

(h) All couples house around. (8 bars)

FIGURE 4 : POLKA (88 BARS)

(a) All couples take waltz hold and dance anticlockwise around the set, ladies reversing and gents dancing forward all the way round. (8 bars)

(b) All couples house around. (8 bars)

(c) The ladies join right hands in the centre, dance across and turn twice with left arms around the opposite gent, then join right hands in the centre again, dance back to place and swing their partners. (16 bars)

(d) Repeat (a) to (c). (32 bars)

(e) Repeat (a) and (b). (16 bars)

FIGURE 5 : SLIDE (232 BARS)

(a) Top couples house around each other. (8 bars)

(b) Top couples slide to the centre, slide back and house across to opposite positions. (8 bars)

(c) Top couples repeat (b), dancing back to place. (8 bars)

(d) Top couples house around each other again. (8 bars)

(e) Top couples repeat (b) to (d). (24 bars)

(f) Side couples dance (a) to (e). (56 bars)

(g) Top couples repeat (a) to (e). (56 bars)

(h) Side couples repeat (a) to (e). (56 bars)

FIGURE 6 : HORNPIPE (160 BARS)

(a) All couples dance the body, dancing hornpipe steps (hop 1 2 3, stamp 1 2 3, when dancing in and back, and hop 1 2 3, hop 1 2 3, when turning clockwise to the next position). (16 bars)

(b) All couples house around. (8 bars)

(c) All advance (hop 1 2 3, hop 1 2 3) and retire in a circle (4 bars), then advance again, and as the gents retire, each lady turns anticlockwise under the left hand of the gent on her right as she passes in front of him to the next lady's position on her right.   (8 bars)

(d) All dance the body with their new partners.   (16 bars)

(e) All house around with their new partners.   (8 bars)

(f) Repeat (c) to (e) three times, ladies dancing with each gent in turn before dancing the last body and housing with their own partners.

                        (96 bars)

WEXFORD HALF-SET

This version of the Wexford Half-Set was given to me by John O'Connor and Mary Walshe of the Castlebridge Set Dancers. They learned the set from Paddy Flynn of Enniscorthy. All dance the Wexford reel step to the polkas and the Wexford jig step to the jigs when dancing on the spot.

FIGURE 1: THE CROSSOVER; POLKA (48 BARS)

(a) Both couples take inside hands and dance on the spot facing the opposite couple. (8 bars)

(b) Both couples cross anticlockwise to opposite positions, with each lady turning clockwise once under her partner's right hand (2 bars), and dance on the spot (6 bars). (8 bars)

(c) Both couples swing in opposite positions (6 bars) and dance out (2 bars). (8 bars)

(d) Both couples repeat (b) and (c), crossing back to finish in their own positions. (16 bars)

FIGURE 2: THE CHAIN; JIG (168 BARS)

(a) Ladies chain with right hands in the centre, take the opposite gent's left hand in their left and dance anticlockwise around him while turning clockwise under his arm. The gent does not turn while the lady is dancing around him. Ladies chain with right hands in the centre again and, taking their own partner's right hand in their left, both couples cross anticlockwise to opposite positions, with each lady turning clockwise once under her partner's right hand. (8 bars)

(b) Both couples take inside hands and dance on the spot facing the opposite couple. (8 bars)

(c) Both couples cross anticlockwise to their own positions, with each lady turning clockwise once under her partner's right hand (2 bars), and dance on the spot (6 bars). (8 bars)

(d) Both couples swing, with the first couple crossing as they swing to leave the lady beside the second couple. (8 bars)

(e) All dance on the spot, with the line of three facing the top gent. (8 bars)

(f) Top gent turns anticlockwise to face out of the set (2 bars) and all dance on the spot (6 bars). (8 bars)

(g) Top gent turns anticlockwise to face the line of three (2 bars) and all dance on the spot again (6 bars). (8 bars)

(h) All swing in a circle of four in the centre, hands around the waist.

(8 bars)

(i) Repeat (a) to (h) with second couple leading. (64 bars)
(j) Repeat (a) to (c). (24 bars)
(k) Both couples swing (6 bars) and dance out (2 bars). (8 bars)

FIGURE 3: SIDESTEP; POLKA (48 BARS)

(a) Both couples take inside hands and dance on the spot facing the opposite couple. (8 bars)
(b) All sidestep past their partners, gents going to the right and passing behind the ladies (2 bars). Taking right hand in right with the opposite person, all dance on the spot (6 bars). (8 bars)
(c) All swing the opposite gent or lady (6 bars) and dance back into their own partner's place, where they finished the sidestep (2 bars). (8 bars)
(d) All sidestep back to their own places and dance out facing their own partners. (8 bars)
(e) All swing their partners (6 bars) and dance out (2 bars). (8 bars)

FIGURE 4: POLKA (88 BARS)

(a) Both couples take inside hands and dance on the spot facing the opposite couple. (8 bars)
(b) Both couples cross anticlockwise to opposite positions, with each lady turning clockwise once under her partner's right hand (2 bars), and dance on the spot (6 bars). (8 bars)
(c) Both couples swing in opposite positions (6 bars) and dance out (2 bars). (8 bars)
(d) Both couples repeat (b) and (c), crossing back to swing in their own positions. (16 bars)
(e) Repeat (a) to (d). (40 bars)

WICKLOW SET

Notes for this set were provided by Angela Fagan from Bray. A written description of it was given to Angela by one of her dancers. The origin of the set is unknown. The set was preceded by the 'grand march'. All couples marched up the centre of the floor, then parted, ladies circling to the right and gents circling to the left. All danced to the back to meet their partners again and continued up the centre with them. This time, when they reached the top of the hall, the first couple circled off to the right, the second couple to the left and so on, all dancing to the back of the hall once more. They now marched up the centre in lines of four. At the top, they formed half-sets across the hall. The dance finished with a grand chain around the hall, with gents going to the right and ladies to the left. When the partners met again, all danced a barn dance.

FIGURE 1: JIG (56 BARS)

(a) Partners take inside hands. The first couple raise their hands to form an arch and both couples cross to opposite positions, with the second couple passing under the arch. All turn in to their partners and take the other hand, then cross back, with the second couple forming the arch this time and the first couple passing under it. (8 bars)

(b) Ladies chain – right hands in the centre, left to the opposite gent, right in the centre again – and dance back to place. (8 bars)

(c) Both couples swing in waltz hold. (8 bars)

(d) Repeat (a) to (c). (24 bar)

FIGURE 2: JIG (56 BARS)

(a) Holding right hand in right, both couples advance and retire twice. (8 bars)

(b) Holding right hand in right, both couples dance anticlockwise around the set, ladies turning clockwise four times under their partner's right hand. (8 bars)

(c) Both couples swing in place. (8 bars)

(d) Repeat (a) to (c). (24 bars)

FIGURE 3: JIG (104 BARS)

(a) Partners take inside hands. First couple raise their hands to form an arch and both couples cross to opposite positions, with the second couple passing under the arch. All turn in to their partners and take the other hand, then cross back, the second couple forming the arch this time and the first couple passing under it.

(8 bars)

(b) Ladies chain – right hands in the centre, left to opposite gent, right in the centre again – and dance back to place, turning around their own partners with their left hands to cross again and swing the opposite gent. (16 bars)

(c) Repeat (a) and (b), all starting with the opposite lady or gent this time and finishing with their own partners. (24 bars)

(d) Repeat (a) to (c). (48 bars)

FIGURE 4: JIG (120 BARS)

(a) Partners take inside hands. First couple raise their hands to form an arch and both couples cross to opposite positions, with the second couple passing under the arch. All turn in to their partners and take the other hand, then cross back, with the second couple forming the arch and the first couple passing under it. (8 bars)

(b) Ladies chain – right hands in the centre, left to opposite gent, right in the centre again – and dance back to place. (8 bars)

(c) While the second couple dance in place, turning twice, the first couple house inside, moving across to leave the lady on the left side of the second gent. He places an arm over each lady's shoulder, taking their hands, while the top gent takes their other hands. (8 bars)

(d) All advance and retire once (4 bars), then ladies change over to the other gent and all advance and retire again. (8 bars)

(e) All swing in four in the centre. (8 bars)

(f) Ladies chain – right hands in the centre, left to opposite gent, right in the centre again – and dance back to place. (8 bars)

(g) Both couples swing in waltz hold. (8 bars)

(h) Repeat (a) to (g) with second couple leading. (56 bars)

WILLIAMSTOWN SET

This set comes from the Roscommon–Galway border area. It has been revived by Mary Whyte, who grew up in Lowberry. Mary has dedicated the set, which was originally danced at crossroads and house dances in the Lowberry and Williamstown areas, to the dancers of previous generations who kept it alive. Recently she has taught it to the Williamstown Set Dancers. My thanks to Mary for giving me the set and also to P. J. Gorevan, who originally told me about it and put me in contact with her.

FIGURE 1: REEL (120 BARS)

(a) All couples lead around anticlockwise, holding crossed hands, and dance the last two bars facing their partners. (8 bars)

(b) All couples swing in waltz hold. (8 bars)

(c) Top ladies dance the slow chain. They dance to the centre, take right hands low and turn once around each other, then give their left hands to the opposite gent and turn once around him. The gents turn too. They repeat the movements back to home. (16 bars)

(d) Top couples swing in place. (8 bars)

(e) Side couples dance (c) and (d). (24 bars)

(f) All gents join left hands in the centre and take their partners right hand in right. Gents keep their left hands in the centre while all dance anticlockwise to the next position on the right, where each lady turns clockwise once under her partner's right arm (4 bars). These movements are repeated as all dance around the set to home (12 bars). (16 bars)

(g) Facing into the set, gents place their right arm around the lady's waist as she places her left hand on the gent's near shoulder. All advance, retire and house to the opposite position. Then they advance, retire and house back to their own positions. (16 bars)

(h) All couples swing in place. (8 bars)

(i) All couples house around. (8 bars)

FIGURE 2: REEL (112 BARS)

(a) All couples lead around anticlockwise, holding crossed hands, and dance the last two bars facing their partners. (8 bars)

(b) All couples swing in waltz hold. (8 bars)

(c) All dancers turn away from their partners to face the person on the

other side in the corner. They dance towards each other into waltz
hold and swing in the corner. (8 bars)

(d) Taking their new partner's right hand in their right, with the lady
on the right-hand side of the gent, all advance and retire twice to
the centre. (8 bars)

(e) Still holding right hand in right and facing each other, each lady
turns clockwise twice under the gent's right arm. (8 bars)

(f) All dance back to their own positions (2 bars), passing right
shoulder to right, and swing their partners in place (6 bars). (8 bars)

(g) Both top couples dance to the centre, with first top couple holding
right hand in right. First top couple raise their right hands to make
an arch and second top couple pass under the arch, with the lady
leading. At the other side, the second top lady turns clockwise into
place while the second top gent turns anticlockwise into place.
When second top couple have passed under the arch, first top
couple lower their hands and turn clockwise, side by side, into the
opposite position. (8 bars)

(h) Top couples repeat (g) as they dance back to their own positions.
This time, second top couple make the arch and first top couple
pass under it. (8 bars)

(i) Both top couples swing in place. (8 bars)

(j) Side couples dance (g) to (i). (24 bars)

(k) All couples house around. (8 bars)

FIGURE 3: REEL (120 BARS)

(a) All couples lead around anticlockwise, holding crossed hands,
and dance the last two bars facing their partners. (8 bars)

(b) All couples swing in waltz hold. (8 bars)

(c) Top ladies chain, taking right hands low in the centre to turn twice
around each other, then dancing back to their own places to face
their partners. (8 bars)

(d) Top couples swing in waltz hold. (8 bars)

(e) Side couples repeat (c) and (d). (16 bars)

(f) All face their own partners and dance back to back. They dance
forward, passing their partner right shoulder to right, dance
sideways to their right, reverse back, passing left shoulder to left,
and dance the last two bars facing their partner. (8 bars)

(g) All couples swing in waltz hold. (8 bars)

(h) Taking their partners right hand in right, top couples face the side
couple on their left and side couples face the top couple on their

right. All couples advance and retire once, then pass through to change places with the other couple. Each lady passes between the opposite couple while the gents pass on the outside. (8 bars)

(i) Repeat (h) three times with top couples dancing clockwise around the set and side couples dancing anticlockwise around it. Each top couple meets each side couple twice as they dance around to home. (24 bars)

(j) All couples swing in waltz hold. (8 bars)

(k) All couples house around. (8 bars)

FIGURE 4: JIG (128 BARS)

(a) All couples lead around anticlockwise, holding crossed hands, and dance the last two bars facing their partners. (8 bars)

(b) All couples swing in waltz hold. (8 bars)

(c) Top couples house around each other. (8 bars)

(d) Top gents cross, passing right shoulder to right, and swing opposite ladies. (8 bars)

(e) Top couples house around with new partners. (8 bars)

(f) Top gents cross, passing right shoulder to right, and swing their own partners. (8 bars)

(g) Top couples house around with their own partners. (8 bars)

(h) Side couples dance (c) to (g). (40 bars)

(i) Taking their partner's right hand in their right, all chain around the set, gents anticlockwise and ladies clockwise (12 bars), then swing their partners (4 bars). (16 bars)

(j) All couples house around. (8 bars)

FIGURE 5: POLKA (136 BARS)

(a) Taking hands in a circle, all advance and retire twice. (8 bars)

(b) All couples swing in waltz hold. (8 bars)

(c) First top couple house inside. (8 bars)

(d) As first top couple finish their house, second top couple move apart from their partners, each dancer joining the nearest side couple in a line of three. First top couple take right hand in right as they face each other and pass each other by, with the top lady giving her left hand to the nearest person in the line on the left-hand side of the first top couple, while the top gent gives his left hand to the nearest person in the line on the right-hand side of the first top couple. Each of them turns anticlockwise around the person in the line and continues to turn clockwise, right hand in right around each other in the centre (4 bars). They repeat the movements, turning with their left hand around the second person in the line and with their right hand around each other again (4 bars). They then turn with left hands around the third person in the line and, taking waltz hold, house back to home and move apart to line up with the nearest side couple (8 bars). (16 bars)

(e) Repeat (c) and (d) with second top couple leading. (24 bars)

(f) Repeat (c) and (d) with first side couple leading, while second side couple line up, each dancer with the nearest top couple.

(24 bars)

(g) Repeat (c) and (d) with first side couple leading, while second side couple line up, each dancer with the nearest top couple.

(24 bars)

(h) All couples swing in waltz hold. (8 bars)

(i) All couples house around. (8 bars)

WOLFHILL SET

I learned this set on 14 May 1997 from Mary Gohery and her dancers in Wolfhill, County Laois. The first four figures are usually danced in half-sets and the fifth figure is danced in a full set. When dancing as a half-set, two or more half-sets join together for the fifth figure.

FIGURE 1 : POLKA (96 BARS)
(a) Holding right hand in right, both couples advance and retire, then cross anticlockwise, and gents turn the lady clockwise to face in at the opposite position. (8 bars)
(b) They repeat (a), crossing back home and turning the lady again. (8 bars)
(c) Both couples swing in place in *céilí* hold. (8 bars)
(d) Ladies chain with right hands in the centre, turn with left hand under the opposite gent's left arm while the gent stays facing in, bringing the hands over the gent's head as the lady completes her turn around him, and dance back, passing right shoulder to shoulder. (8 bars)
(e) Both couples house around each other. (8 bars)
(f) Advance and retire twice, right hand in right. (8 bars)
(g) Swing in place. (8 bars)
(h) Repeat (d) to (g). (32 bars)

FIGURE 2 : JIG (104 BARS)
(a) Holding right hand in right, both couples dance battering steps in place. (8 bars)
(b) Both couples dance to the position on the right, turn the lady clockwise on the spot, then dance into opposite position and turn the lady again. (8 bars)
(c) Repeat (a) and (b), dancing back to place. (16 bars)
(d) Holding right hand in right, both couples dance battering steps in place. (8 bars)
(e) Both couples swing. (8 bars)
(f) Repeat (a) to (e). (48 bars)

FIGURE 3 : POLKA (112 BARS)
(a) Holding right hands, both couples advance and retire twice. (8 bars)
(b) Top lady and opposite gent dance forward left shoulder to left,

turn clockwise to face each other from the other side, dance back left shoulder to left and turn clockwise to face each other from their own side. (8 bars)

(c) Top lady and opposite gent swing in the centre. (8 bars)

(d) The four dancers form a circle in the centre, all holding hands, and the ladies dance on the spot with their hands crossed (8 bars). Ladies turn clockwise and all keep dancing in the circle (8 bars).

(16 bars)

(e) Both couples reverse to home positions holding hands, dance on the spot, then advance and retire once. (8 bars)

(f) Both couples swing. (8 bars)

(g) Repeat (b) to (f). (48 bars)

FIGURE 4 : POLKA (152 BARS)

(a) Both couples take inside hands as in the Threshing Set and cross to opposite side, the first couple making an arch and the second couple passing under it. At the other side all turn in to their partners, take the other hand and cross back. This time, the second couple make the arch and the first couple pass under it. (8 bars)

(b) Ladies chain, as in Figure 1. (8 bars)

(c) Both couples house around in waltz hold. (8 bars)

(d) Both couples advance and retire twice, holding right hands. (8 bars)

(e) First couple swing up – cross the set while swinging to meet the second couple, who stand with the gent's arm around the lady's waist and her hand on his shoulder. (8 bars)

(f) Swing in four, first to the left (8 bars), then to the right (8 bars). Ladies place their hands on the gents' shoulders. (16 bars)

(g) Both couples retire to place, dance on the spot, then advance and retire once. (8 bars)

(h) Both couples swing in place. (8 bars)

(i) Repeat (a) to (h) with second couple leading. (72 bars)

FIGURE 5 : JIG OR POLKA (200 BARS)

(a) Top couples advance and retire, arm around the waist, then cross anticlockwise to face in on the other side. (8 bars)

(b) Advance, retire and cross back. (8 bars)

(c) Side couples dance (a) and (b). (16 bars)

(d) All circle, advance and retire twice, ladies moving on to the right. (8 bars)

(e) All swing new partners. (8 bars)

(f) Repeat (a) to (e) until ladies are swinging their own partners. (144 bars)

BIBLIOGRAPHY

Breathnach, Breandán. *Dancing in Ireland*. Dal gCais Publications, Milltown Malbay, County Clare, 1983.

Breathnach, Breandán. *Folk Music and Dances of Ireland*. Mercier Press, Cork & Dublin, 1989.

Buckman, Peter. *Let's Dance*. Paddington Press Ltd, London, 1978.

Curtis, P. J. *Notes from the Heart*. Torc, Dublin, 1994.

Donnelly, Sean. *Ceol na hÉireann*. Na Píobairí Uilleann, Dublin, 1993.

Flett, J. P. & T. M. *Traditional Dancing in Scotland*. Routledge & Kegan Paul, London, 1953.

Grattan-Flood, W. H. *A History of Irish Music*. Browne & Nolan Ltd, Dublin, 1927.

O'Keeffe, J. G., and O'Brien, Art. *A Handbook of Irish Dances*. Gill & Macmillan, Dublin, 1902.

O'Neill, Francis. *Irish Folk Music*. Regan Printing House, Chicago, 1910.

Sachs, Curt. *World History of the Dance*. W. W. Norton & Co Inc, 1937.

Scott, Edward. *Dancing as an Art and Pastime*. George Bell & Sons, London, 1892.

Tubridy, Michael. *Connie Ryan: The Mighty Set Dancing Master*. Privately published, Offaly, 1999.